After these things I looked, and behold, a door standing open in heaven. And the first voice which I heard was like a trumpet speaking with me, saying, "Come up here, and I will show you things which must take place after this." Revelation 4:1

Copyright © 2011 by Johnny Morales

GLOBAL PROPHETIC TRAINING

Published by
Prophetic Streams Network
Las Vegas, NV

ISBN 978-0-615-29416-2
Printed in the USA

All rights reserved. This book is protected by the copyright laws of the United States of America. The use of short quotations or occasional page copying for personal or group study is permitted and encouraged. Permission will be granted upon request. Unless otherwise identified, Scripture quotations are from the New King James Version of the Bible©1972, 1980, 1982, Thomas Nelson Inc., publishers. Used by permission. "Scripture taken form The Message. Copyright© 1993,1994, 1995, 1996, 2000, 2001, 2002. Used by permission of NavPress Publishing Group." No part of this book may be reproduced or transmitted in any from or by any means without written permission from the publisher.

Photography by Cara Terraccianno
Cover design by Prophetic Streams Network & David Salazar

Foreword

I have been in the ministry for over 55+ years and I have had the honor of working with prophetic healing ministers such as A.A. Allen and other great prophetic ministers of the faith; I am delighted to see how Johnny through his manual is sharing keys of prophetic revelation for unlocking the gift of prophecy within those who he ministers to. Johnny shares basic biblical foundational truths to hearing the voice of God. This will help those who are hungry to hear God's voice more clearly as well as training them to be an oracle of God. God said, 'And it shall come to pass in the last days, says God, That I will pour out of My Spirit on all flesh; Your sons and your daughters shall prophesy, Your young men shall see visions, your old men shall dream dreams. And on My menservants and on My maidservants I will pour out My Spirit in those days; And they shall prophesy. Acts 2:17-18

Global Prophetic Training manual is a must read for those who want to be a source of encouragement, comfort and edification to both the body of Christ and to a lost and dying world.

Apostle Don Stewart
Don Stewart Association

What is the prophetic? Why is it important? Is the prophetic really for today? The manual you are holding in your hands lays the groundwork for understanding and walking out the key prophetic principles necessary for impacting our world for Jesus Christ. Johnny Morales is not only a Pastor and a friend; he is one of the most Godcentered man I know. He has dedicated himself to the work of equipping, activating, and imparting a prophetic movement of God within the body of Christ. He has imparted into me and into my family in such a powerful way. Now, with this manual, you will be the recipient of this prophetic impartation also.

I had the opportunity to earn my Doctorate of Strategic Leadership from Regent University's School of Global Leadership and Entrepreneurship. Although I admit that the education afforded me by the school was top in the field, it was only when I partnered that education with the prophetic training I received from my church, that I could embrace the essence of successful godly leadership.

Whether you are new to the prophetic or you have a vast array of prophetic experience, this manual will certainly take you to the next level. It can be used individually or in a group setting and I strongly encourage you to use it to train every Christian in your ministry. If you are ready to jumpstart the prophetic move of God in your ministry, this manual is the ideal place to start!

Joni Reid, DSL, MSW, CW
Las Vegas, NV

Endorsements

"Every believer needs to be able to hear and share the voice of God. Johnny Morales' book 'Global Prophetic Training' brings a simple yet powerful revelation to equip believers to be doers of prophetic ministry. Everyone should read this book so they can begin to minister the voice of God to an anxious world that is hungry for His presence."

Timothy Hamon, PhD
CEO, Christian International Ministries

"Johnny Morales has done an awesome job outlining what it takes to be in the prophetic movement to equip, activate, and impart to those eager to learn. We highly endorse Johnny's manual "GLOBAL PROPHETIC TRAINING" for any ministry that wants a strong foundation to operate in the prophetic with sound doctrine. Johnny has used both corporate and personal examples from his 20+ years of ministry."

Allen and Francine Fosdick
Founders/Visionaries, People of Prophetic Power Ministries,
Upfront in the prophetic Media Ministries, White Horse
Training and Retreat Center, & Destiny Life Solution LLC.

TABLE OF CONTENTS

Title   **Page**

Foreword……………………………………………………….2

Endorsements………………………………………………….3

Acknowledgement……………………………………………..5

Introduction…………………………………………………….6

Chapter 1 The Secret Revealed………………………………8

Chapter 2 The Prophetic Waves of the Holy Spirit……………26

Chapter 3 Hearing the Voice of God………………………….36

Chapter 4 Understanding Prophecy……………………………58

Chapter 5 Sharing the Voice of God…………………………..76

Chapter 6 The Prophetic Ministry …………………………….90

Chapter 7 The Restoration of the Prophetic Ministry …………102

Chapter 8 Ezekiel's Prophetic River…………………………..114

Chapter 9 The Language of God's Heart……………………..130

Notes……………………………………………………….144

Prophetic Journal……………………………………………146

Acknowledgment

I am grateful for the encouragement and love from my family and friends in Christ. This is truly a dream in the making. My family and I have had the privilege and opportunity to receive life-changing impartations throughout the last 25+ years from both men and woman of God who have given of their time love and care both in the word and by the Spirit of the Lord. I would like to thank some special friends Pastor Ray Reeder, Pastors Robert and Carol Bouchard, John Kenney, Michelle Padgett, John C. Maxwell, Pastors Paul and Denise Goulet, Pasqual and Norma Urrabazo, Joel and Robyn Garcia, Sergio and Kathy Scataglini. I'm also thankful for others who have imparted into my life such as; Dr. Chuck Pierce, Bishop Bill Hamon, Dr. Lance Wallnau, Bill Johnson, Kris Vallotton, Claudio Freidzon, Steve Thompson, Rick Joyner, Randy Clark, Heidi Baker, Lou Engle, Sean Smith, Peter Wagner and the faculty of Wagner Leadership Institute as well as Pastors Jose and Toni Boveda and Apostle Don Stewart.

Finally, I am so thankful to God who has adopted me into His heart as one of many sons. As a result of His love being poured into my life, I have spent 25 years learning and seeking the heart of the Father. As described in Malachi Chapter 4:5-6 we will see the generations aligned with His word: 5 ***"Behold, I will send you Elijah the prophet before the coming of the great and dreadful day of the LORD. 6 And he will turn the hearts of the fathers to the children, and the hearts of the children to their fathers, lest I come and strike the earth with a curse."***

INTRODUCTION

³ The voice of one crying in the wilderness: "Prepare the way of the LORD; Make straight in the desert A highway for our God. ⁴ Every valley shall be exalted And every mountain and hill brought low; The crooked places shall be made straight And the rough places smooth; ⁵ The glory of the LORD shall be revealed, And all flesh shall see it together; for the mouth of the LORD has spoken." Isaiah 40:3-5

The purpose and function of prophets, prophecy, prophetic schools and the prophetic ministry continue to be a vital part of God's global plan for His people. God's people are revealed in scripture as the temple of the Holy Spirit, the body of Christ, sons and daughters, and as the bride of Christ. His people are now in the process of being refined, purified, and matured as the bride of Christ, so that she is ready for His soon return.

What a joyous celebration it will be at the great wedding feast prepared in heaven for the marriage supper of the Lamb. Until this celebration happens in heaven, there will be a release of the sound of a global company of prophets and prophetic people in the earth. They will help prepare the way of the Lord and help to make ready a bride who will be without spot or blemish. You have been chosen by God as one who will be His voice of Love to both the world and to the church.

Yes, and all the prophets, from Samuel and those who follow, as many as have spoken, have also foretold these days. ²⁵ You are sons of the prophets, and of the covenant which God made with our fathers, saying to Abraham, 'And in your seed all the families of the earth shall be blessed.'¹¹² Acts 3:24-25

Sons of the Prophets

Since the time of Samuel's school of the prophets (1 Sam 10:5; 1 Sam 19:19-20) until now, there have been true "schools of the prophets". These schools are helping God's people learn to hear the voice of God and become the voice of God to their families, friends, neighbors, workplaces, churches, and their world. Jesus prophesied that false prophets will arise in the last days, but I believe that God's solution involves the true prophets of God arising in this hour. Jesus also told His disciples a parable of the tares and the wheat to show that there will be both true and false ministry.

> *²⁴ Another parable He put forth to them, saying: "The kingdom of heaven is like a man who sowed good seed in his field; ²⁵ but while men slept, his enemy came and sowed tares among the wheat and went his way. ²⁶ But when the grain had sprouted and produced a crop, then the tares also appeared. ²⁷ So the servants of the owner came and said to him, 'Sir, did you not sow good seed in your field? How then does it have tares?' ²⁸ He said to them, 'An enemy has done this.' The servants said to him, 'Do you want us then to go and gather them up?' ²⁹ But he said, 'No, lest while you gather up the tares you also uproot the wheat with them. ³⁰ Let both grow together until the harvest, and at the time of harvest I will say to the reapers, "First gather together the tares and bind them in bundles to burn them, but gather the wheat into my barn." Matthew 13:24-30*

God is releasing His true company of prophets and prophetic people in this day that will point the way to Jesus and sow good seed in His field. True prophetic schools, training, and activation are something that is needed within the church around the world. This will help to counter-attack the false weeds that try to deceive even the elect. Through this Global Prophetic Training manual, it is my prayer that you will receive good seed, fresh wisdom, revelation, knowledge and an impartation of the Sprit of the Lord, to go to the next level of your prophetic potential.

Gross spiritual darkness is invading the earth's atmosphere to keep people from seeing the beauty of God's love, redemption, and eternal purposes; however, the word of the Lord is illuminating the darkness just as Isaiah prophesied in Isaiah 60:1. **"Arise and shine for your light has come and glory of the Lord is risen upon you"**. Even in the midst of the gross darkness, the light of global prophetic revelation will break forth in the life of the church and many will come to that light and see God's glory, love, redemption, and His plans for His people.

Johnny Morales

CHAPTER 1
THE SECRET REVEALED

I know what I'm doing. I have it all planned out—plans to take care of you, not abandon you, plans to give you the future you hope for. Jeremiah 29:11 (MSG)

NOTES

➢ FOUNDATIONAL TRUTHS ABOUT THE SECRETS OF GOD

1. **God wants his people to know His heart, plans and thoughts.** He wants to bring clarity of understanding for the times and the seasons that you and I are living in. God is revealed as the Chief Shepherd and His people as the sheep. *[27] My sheep hear My voice, and I know them, and they follow Me. John 10:27.* In Psalms 23, God is revealed as a good shepherd who takes care of His sheep and leads them in places of refreshing, rest, nourishment, anointing, security, goodness, and mercy. God does not hide things "from us", He hides things "for us". Those who seek after the Lord and call upon His name will be the ones whom God will show great and mighty things.

   Jeremiah 33:3 shows us how to tap into supernatural revelation of God which will cause us to know what He is doing in our own life and the world around us. God tells the prophet Jeremiah in the midst of his difficult circumstances, *'Call to Me, and I will answer you, and show you great and mighty things, which you do not know.'* This prophetic promise is something that you can take a hold of for your life today. I see three keys of revelation in this passage of scripture:

   - **"Call upon me":** This is God's voice calling out to you and giving you a simple instruction on what to do. It is our responsibility to respond to His voice and begin to call upon Him in prayer.

   - **"I will answer you":** When we call upon God we must believe and expect to hear Him answer us. This is God's promise to you when you take the initiative to call upon Him and seek Him with all your heart. Calling upon God is something that you can do on a daily basis until the answer is received. Some have taught that it shows a lack of faith if we pray for something more than once. I disagree with this type of thinking, because it is contrary to what Jesus Himself taught His disciples in the parable of the persistent widow. Read Luke 18:1-8.

   - **"Show you great and mighty things which you do not know":** As God's children you can receive what He desires to show you. God will begin to open your vision to seeing beyond your situation and your own personal life struggles. Do not allow your current situation, or personal trials to keep you from seeking, believing, and then receiving from His perspective. This is what will separate the eagles from the chickens. The chicken only can see what's in front of it and it is usually looking down at the ground. An eagle has the ability to soar above the storms and see beyond the horizon into the radiant sun. You were meant to soar like an eagle, seeing life from a heavenly perspective.

2. **God reveals His secrets with those called His friends.** The friends of God will be those to whom God reveals the deepest secrets of His very own heart. John the Baptist, who was a prophet, declared something that must be priority for any prophet or in any prophetic movement, which is found in John 3:28-29. *²⁹ He who has the bride is the bridegroom; but the friend of the bridegroom, who stands and hears him, rejoices greatly because of the bridegroom's voice.*

3. **Friends of God are those who have both the willingness and the obedience to serve Him with a pure heart.** Jesus reveals that a true friend will lay down his very own life for the sake of the other. Jesus is the best example of how a friend should be.*¹³ Greater love has no one than this, than to lay down one's life for his friends.¹⁴ You are My friends if you do whatever I command you. John 15:13-14*

   There are biblical examples, in the Old and New Testament, of individuals whose hearts were after God's own heart and were considered a friend of God. God shows these types of friends what He is doing in their personal lives, families, workplaces, their churches and the world in which they live. These individuals include people like:

   - Abraham
   - Joseph
   - David
   - Job
   - The major and minor prophets
   - John the Baptist
   - The disciples of Christ
   - The Apostle Paul

 # NOTES

4. **Intimacy is the key for unlocking the secrets of God's heart, mind, will, and emotions.** The word intimacy can also be defined as "in to me you see". God wants His people to know Him not just intellectually, but experientially from the heart. Jesus reveals the sobering truth of what its like to do ministry using His name, His gifting, His talents and yet have no intimate relationship with Him in Matthew 7:21-23 *[21] "Not everyone who says to Me, 'Lord, Lord,' shall enter the kingdom of heaven, but he who does the will of My Father in heaven. [22] Many will say to Me in that day, 'Lord, Lord, have we not prophesied in Your name, cast out demons in Your name, and done many wonders in Your name?' [23] And then I will declare to them, 'I never knew you; depart from Me, you who practice lawlessness!'*

5. **Understanding the four rooms of intimacy with God.** Sons and daughters of God have been granted access to the most intimate places in God. These places, which I call "chambers", are the very rooms reserved for His bride. Prophets and the prophetic ministry also serve as doorkeepers to these places in God and their job is to open the door of revelation into these rooms so that God's people can also access these chambers themselves. *[4] Draw me away!* THE DAUGHTERS OF JERUSALEM *We will run after you.* THE SHULAMITE *The king has brought me into his chambers.* THE DAUGHTERS OF JERUSALEM *We will be glad and rejoice in you. We will remember your love more than wine. Song of Solomon 1:4*

   A. **The Chamber of His Heart:**
   David is a great example of how a person can actually win the heart of God. His heart after God was able to unlock a family legacy for the generations to come. King David captured the heart of God, even in his youth, while tending His father's sheep. David's heart devotion to God from his youth was what propelled him into being one of the greatest leaders in the history of Israel. The Global prophetic movement must have God's heart as priority at all times. Whatever is done should be done with integrity and a motive that is pleasing to the heart of God. The fear of man and man-pleasing can not be mixed with the prophetic ministry; otherwise it becomes contaminated with eventual disobedience to God. In 1 Samuel 15: 24, we see the end result of Saul's fear of man. *[24] Then Saul said to Samuel, "I have sinned, for I have transgressed the commandment of the LORD and your words, because I feared the people and obeyed their voice.*

B. **The Chamber of His mind:**
Can you imagine having access into the creative mind of God whoes every thought is constantly pure, upright, and good? In Psalm 139, David writes that the very thoughts of God about him outnumber the very sands of the seashore. That is awesome! Paul writes to the church in Philippi and reveals that we have the mind of Christ. Jesus has made it possible for you to receive a new mind called the mind of Christ. This gives us accesses into God's strategies, plans, and intents for our own life and the life of others around us. How would you like God to first talk with you about something He is thinking about before He acts? Abraham, who is known as the friend of God, had revelation of God's mind concerning an entire city. *[17] And the LORD said, "Shall I hide from Abraham what I am doing, [18] since Abraham shall surely become a great and mighty nation, and all the nations of the earth shall be blessed in him? Genesis 18:17-18*

C. **The Chamber of God's Will:**
God has created every human being with a free will. With this free will, people can choose to do right or wrong, good or evil, blessings or cursing. When we enter the chamber of God's will, we will see that it is His will that has our best interest at heart. Many walk about in complete uncertainty concerning the will of God for their life. Others walk in complete disobedience, simply rejecting the will of God for their life. True intimacy with God will cause the will of man to come into complete submission based on love. The call of prophets and the prophetic movement is to know and do the will of God. *[1] Therefore, I urge you, brothers, in view of God's mercy, to offer your bodies as living sacrifices, holy and pleasing to God--this is your spiritual act of worship. [2] Do not conform any longer to the pattern of this world, but be transformed by the renewing of your mind. Then you will be able to test and approve what God's will is--his good, pleasing and perfect will. Romans 12:1-2. (NIV)*

Jesus is the greatest example of walking in complete obedience to the will of His Father even though there was great suffering and even death on a cross. Jesus knew the suffering He would have to endure would be temporal and that He

 # NOTES

would soon be sitting on a royal throne next to His Father having secured complete victory over death, hell and the grave. *⁸And being found in appearance as a man, He humbled Himself and became obedient to the point of death, even the death of the cross. ⁹ Therefore God also has highly exalted Him and given Him the name which is above every name, ¹⁰ that at the name of Jesus every knee should bow, of those in heaven, and of those on earth, and of those under the earth, ¹¹ and that every tongue should confess that Jesus Christ is Lord, to the glory of God the Father.* Philippians 2:8-11. The cost of following Jesus and being obedient to His voice will be tested in times of persecution, suffering, and during the intense warfare. Jesus gives a prophetic promise for believers who endure such trials. *¹⁰ Blessed are those who are persecuted for righteousness' sake, For theirs is the kingdom of heaven. ¹¹ "Blessed are you when they revile and persecute you, and say all kinds of evil against you falsely for My sake. ¹² Rejoice and be exceedingly glad, for great is your reward in heaven, for so they persecuted the prophets who were before you.* Matthew 5:10-12.

D. **The Chambers of His Emotions:**
This is something that those walking in intimacy with Him will begin to experience in their life. God is a loving Father whom the scriptures reveal in Hebrews as a High Priest who sympathizes with our weaknesses. God is not a piece of steel in the sky. God revealed Himself through His son Jesus Christ. When God visited Moses in the burning bush, He told Moses that He had seen their misery and heard their cries and this is what moved God to take action and bring deliverance to the entire nation of Israel. It took a man named Moses who would share his feelings and receive the call of God. Jesus is described as one who offered up prayers with loud cries and tears. The bible shows Jesus sharing in the sorrows of tears at the news of His friend Lazarus' death. The prophet Isaiah understood and heard the emotions of God for his people as a cry rang out in the heavens for a back slidden nation, "who will go for us"! Real intimacy with God will cause an emotional response in the heart of God and in our own lives. The Holy Spirit helps you in these times to feel the very compassion of Christ for others causing you to reach out and bring healing to others through your words and actions of Love. Are you willing to share in God's emotions? Remember, He is not an angry God, but a heavenly Father who is actually in a good mood.

6. **Why emotional health is necessary.** I would recommend that every person who desires to walk in the prophetic ministry be open to receive help, healing, and break through for their personal lives. Traumatic experiences such as death, divorce, molestation, child abuse, rape, abandonment, or being hurt by church leadership should be processed through with the help of the Holy Spirit as well as experienced and trained Holy Spirit filled counselors. Many times, we try to deal with these life experiences and tragedies alone; however, we must realize that we were created as a many member body and when one member of the body is hurt there is the support of the other parts of the body that will help. Lack of knowledge, pride, fear, and shame are many times hindrances to us asking for help with our emotional well being. Usually pride, fear, and shame will keep you from processing through these issues of life. God promise for our healing and wholeness is found in 2 Chronicles 7:14: [14] *if My people who are called by My name will humble themselves, and pray and seek My face, and turn from their wicked ways, then I will hear from heaven, and will forgive their sin and heal their land.* True humility and obedience will keep you on the path of healing and blessings.

The Vat Principle

[7] But we have this treasure in earthen vessels, that the excellence of the power may be of God and not of us. 2 Corinthians 4:7

This is an amazing passage of scripture as it applies to every believer in Christ. We are called earthen vessels that contain a great treasure. The treasure is the Lord Jesus Christ. As earthen vessels we must watch over our life so that it remains intact and filled with the pure river of the Holy Spirit. Our hearts and minds are like a large container or vat that stores all of our life experiences. If we are going to be the voice of God to others around us, then we must take diligent care over our hearts and minds (vat) so that they are renewed, clean, and healthy. This is our responsibility with the help of the Holy Spirit inside of us.

If the vat is contaminated with things such as unresolved hurt, pride, unforgiveness, fear of man, rejection, people pleasing, and sins of the flesh, our vats will then become like a muddy swamp. Jesus said that rivers of living water are to flow out of our hearts. If we do not confront these issues from our past, sooner or later the result will be character defects that will eventually bring more hurt, shame and humiliation to ourselves and others around us.

Pastor Paul Goulet writes about the vat principal in the Vision Bible (page 18-19). Dr. Richard Dobbins once said, "You do not live with the facts of your life, but the interpretation of the facts of your life." Pastor Paul also writes; we receive most information through our senses, consciously. All of our facts are then filtered through our subconscious reservoir of positively-charged and negatively-charged memories of events and circumstances. Your conscious mind is like the software in your computer. Your subconscious mind is your hard drive. In most cases, the problems in our lives are caused by faulty hardware, filled with viruses and bugs. The Holy Spirit wants to help us clean out our hard drives, so that clear visions may be re-established.

In order to have the ability to clearly understand and interpret our everyday lives, it is crucial that we allow the Holy Spirit to change the way we speak, think and understand (1 Corinthians 13:11-12). The Holy Spirit will:

- *Process emotionally-charged memories through prayer*
- *Help us to confront our past*
- *Re-interpret our memories from an adult perspective*
- *Seek the help of pastors and counselors or friends, to overcome troubling memories.*

YOUR VAT[1]

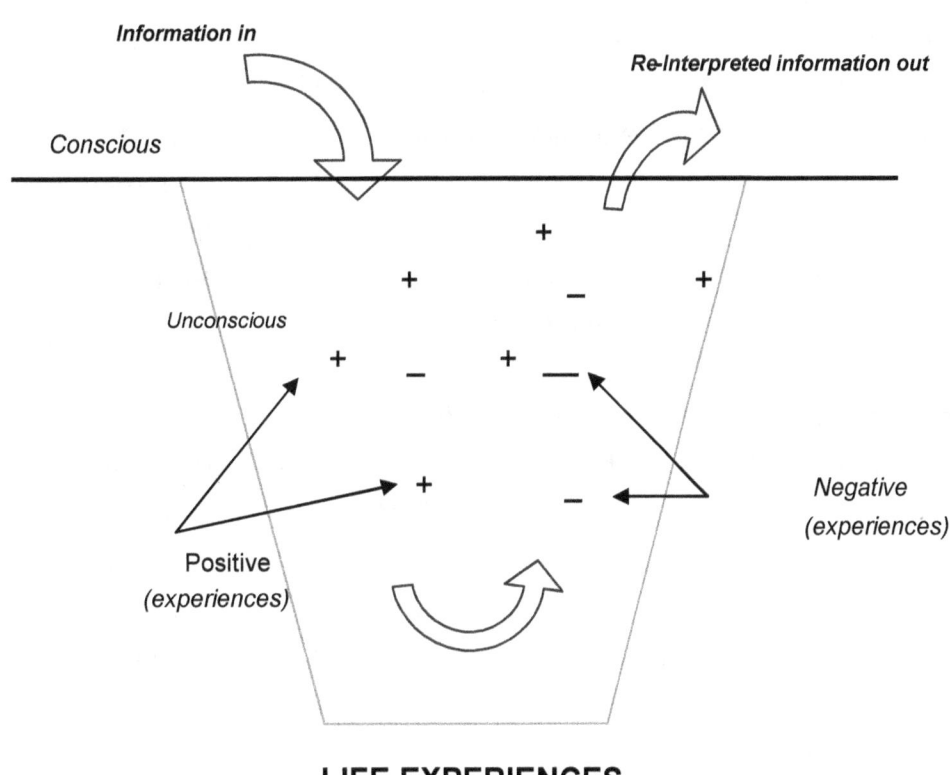

LIFE EXPERIENCES

---

[1] The Vision Bible, (2007). Thomas Nelson: Nashville, TN. p. 19.

God wants to turn bitter water into something that is sweet.
Joseph is a great example of how to maintain a healthy interpretation of all the negative and abusive issues of his past. Instead of becoming "bitter" against his brother and God, he instead became "better". Joseph made a statement that reveals to us how he was able to keep his heart sweet and uncontaminated; He said, "*Do not be afraid, for am I in the place of God? But as for you, you meant evil against me; but God meant it for good, in order to bring it about as it is this day, to save many people alive. Now therefore, do not be afraid; I will provide for you and your little ones." And he comforted them and spoke kindly to them. Genesis 50:19-21*. After being hurt and betrayed by his own brothers Joseph was able to trust God and see his life experience through the eyes of God. Joseph had an opportunity to take revenge against those who had hurt him, but instead he kept his heart clean and uncontaminated from bitterness. We must keep in mind the teaching of Jesus concerning this subject of forgiveness and un-forgiveness.

Then Peter came to Him and said, "Lord, how often shall my brother sin against me, and I forgive him? Up to seven times?" Jesus said to him, "I do not say to you, up to seven times, but up to seventy times seven. Therefore the kingdom of heaven is like a certain king who wanted to settle accounts with his servants. And when he had begun to settle accounts, one was brought to him who owed him ten thousand talents. But as he was not able to pay, his master commanded that he be sold, with his wife and children and all that he had, and that payment be made. The servant therefore fell down before him, saying, 'Master, have patience with me, and I will pay you all.' Then the master of that servant was moved with compassion, released him, and forgave him the debt. "But that servant went out and found one of his fellow servants who owed him a hundred denarii; and he laid hands on him and took him by the throat, saying, 'Pay me what you owe!' So his fellow servant fell down at his feet and begged him, saying, 'Have patience with me, and I will pay you all.' And he would not, but went and threw him into prison till he should pay the debt. So when his fellow servants saw what had been done, they were very grieved, and came and told their master all that had been done. Then his master, after he had called him, said to him, 'You wicked servant! I forgave you all that debt because you begged me. Should you not also have had compassion on your fellow servant, just as I had pity on you?' And his master was angry, and delivered him to the torturers until he should pay all that was due to him. "So My heavenly Father also will do to you if each of you, from his heart, does not forgive his brother his trespasses." Matthew 18:21-35. **Read Exodus 15:22-27.**

-GROUP DISCUSSION-

1. Do you consider yourself a friend of God? Explain.

2. Jesus made it clear that a good tree is known by its fruit and not charisma, gifting, or ability to prophesy. What fruit do you recognize in your own life?

3. What are the chambers of God's heart that you are most familiar with?

4. What is your level of willingness to experience all 4 chambers of intimacy with God?

5. What have you done and what are you willing to do to allow your vat to be cleansed and healed so that fresh rivers of living water can flow from it (i.e., see a counselor, or attend support groups to position your life for an emotional break through)?

- ACTIVATION -

- ✓ **Begin a personal journal to start writing down the revelations that you receive in the intimacy chambers with God. For the next 21 days begin daily to write down what God is saying to you.** *(Note: Just write down whatever comes to mind, without first trying to judge or analyze it in your mind.)*

- ✓ **Make a commitment to develop a daily discipline of the reading of His word**

- ✓ **Humble yourself under the mighty hand of God and ask for help.**

- ✓ **Ask God to begin to help you heal and re-interpret the pains of the past.**

- ✓ **Receive a new wineskin so that you can contain the "new wine" of His Love**

- ✓ **Receive forgiveness and healing from the trauma of the past as you open up to God and others.**

- LIFE APPLICATION -

It is God's plan for His children to be whole spiritually, emotionally, relationally, and physically. Walking out your life with Christ is an "in to me, see" (intimacy) experience. Allow Jesus to be your best friend. He wants to share the secrets of His heart with you.

CHAPTER 2
THE PROPHETIC WAVES OF THE HOLY SPIRIT

*But Peter, standing up with the eleven, raised his voice and said to them, "Men of Judea and all who dwell in Jerusalem, let this be known to you, and heed my words. ⁱ⁵ For these are not drunk, as you suppose, since it is only the third hour of the day. ¹⁶ But this is what was spoken by the prophet Joel: ¹⁷ 'And it shall come to pass in the last days, says God, That I will pour out of My Spirit on all flesh; Your sons and your daughters shall **prophesy**, Your young men shall see visions, Your old men shall dream dreams. ¹⁸ And on My menservants and on My maidservants I will pour out My Spirit in those days; And they shall **prophesy**. Acts 2:14-18*

 # NOTES

➤ FOUNDATIONAL TRUTHS OF THE HOLY SPIRIT AND PROPHECY

1. **The baptism of the Holy Spirit is the key to unlocking prophecy in the church and in the world.** You will begin to prophesy when the Holy Spirit is actively working in your life. As you walk with an intimate knowledge and fellowship of the Holy Spirit, He will be the helper in releasing prophetic ministry to others around you. You will actually begin to see and foresee events before they even happen. Prophecy is not only a gift of the Spirit, but it is a part of His Sovereign nature and characteristics just like Jesus taught. *[13] However, when He, the Spirit of truth, has come, He will guide you into all truth; for He will not speak on His own authority, but whatever He hears He will speak; and He will tell you things to come. John 16:13*

   [26] But the Helper, the Holy Spirit, whom the Father will send in My name, He will teach you all things, and bring to your remembrance all things that I said to you. John 14:26

2. **Tongues and Prophecy are signs to both believers and non believers.** *[20] Brethren, do not be children in understanding; however, in malice be babes, but in understanding be mature. [21] In the law it is written: "With men of other tongues and other lips I will speak to this people; And yet, for all that, they will not hear Me," says the Lord. [22] Therefore tongues are for a sign, not to those who believe but to unbelievers; but prophesying is not for unbelievers but for those who believe. 1 Corinthians 14:20-22*

3. **One of the biblical signs of a true outpouring in the church is the release of tongues and prophecy.** *[18] And on My menservants and on My maidservants I will pour out My Spirit in those days; And they shall prophesy...Acts 2:18.* In the book of Acts when the believers where filled with the Holy Spirit they began to speak in Tongues and prophesied. *[6] And when Paul had laid hands on them, the Holy Spirit came upon them, and they spoke with tongues and prophesied. [7] Now the men were about twelve in all. Acts 19:6-7 (NKJV).* The Apostle writes about tongues and prophecy being signs to both believers and non believers. The powerful result of prophecy is that it will cause even the unbelievers to glorify God and draw them closer to God. *[24] But if all prophesy, and an unbeliever or an uninformed person*

comes in, he is convinced by all, he is convicted by all. ²⁵ And thus the secrets of his heart are revealed; and so, falling down on his face, he will worship God and report that God is truly among you. 1 Corinthians 14:24-25

4. **There is fresh new outpouring of the Holy Spirit that is being poured out upon the church.** A significant supernatural moment in time was when the Holy Spirit filled the 120 believers in the Book of Acts. This was a personal prophecy by Jesus to His disciples. This same prophetic word is still true for the church today. *⁴⁹ "And now I will send the Holy Spirit, just as my Father promised. But stay here in the city until the Holy Spirit comes and fills you with power from heaven." Luke 24:49 (NLT)*

²⁶ "But when the Helper comes, whom I shall send to you from the Father, the Spirit of truth who proceeds from the Father, He will testify of Me. John 15:26

⁷ Nevertheless I tell you the truth. It is to your advantage that I go away; for if I do not go away, the Helper will not come to you; but if I depart, I will send Him to you. John 16:7

5. **The Holy Spirit helps to fulfill His word.** It is important to understand how vital the role of the Holy Spirit is in biblical prophecy and the prophetic movement of God. Since the creation of the world, the Holy Spirit has played an active role in fulfilling the word of God. In Genesis 1:2, the Holy Spirit was brooding over the waters waiting to act upon the spoken words of God the Father. In the very creation account of Genesis you read the words and "God said let there be..." and there was a fulfillment of the very specific words that came out of His mouth. *Then God said, "Let there be light"; and there was light. Genesis 1:3.* The very conception and birth of our Lord and Savior Jesus Christ involved words of prophecy and the Spirit of God. *³¹ And behold, you will conceive in your womb and bring forth a Son, and shall call His name JESUS. Luke 1:31 ³⁴ Then Mary said to the angel, "How can this be, since I do not know a man?" ³⁵ And the angel answered and said to her, "The Holy Spirit will come upon you, and the power of the Highest will overshadow you; therefore, also, that Holy One who is to be born will be called the Son of God." Luke 1:34-35*

6. **The church must maintain a healthy balance with Holy Spirit and the study of scriptures.**

    - A Believer in Christ who only has the written words of prophetic truth in the bible without having an intimate relationship with the Holy Spirit will eventually **dry up**.

    - A Believer in Christ who only has the Spirit of God, but lacks knowledge and neglects reading the prophetic truths in the bible, will eventually **blow up**.

    - A Believer in Christ who has both the written word of prophetic truths found in the bible and an intimate relationship with the Holy Spirit will eventually **grow up**.

7. **Expect a manifestation of the Holy Spirit confirming His word with signs, wonders, and miracle healing.** The coming of the Holy Spirit on the day of Pentecost is the cause for a global wave of the Gospel of the kingdom with a demonstration of healing, signs, and wonders. A Spirit filled life will produce prophecy in the church. *[18] And on My menservants and on My maidservants I will pour out My Spirit in those days; And **they shall prophesy**...Acts 2:18. [17] And these signs will follow those who believe: In My name they will cast out demons; they will speak with new tongues; [18] they will take up serpents; and if they drink anything deadly, it will by no means hurt them; they will lay hands on the sick, and they will recover." [19] So then, after the Lord had spoken to them, He was received up into heaven, and sat down at the right hand of God. [20] And they went out and preached everywhere, the Lord working with them and confirming the word through the accompanying signs. Amen. Mark 16:17-20*

PERSONAL TESTIMONY

After giving my life completely over to Jesus Christ in December of 1986, I was attending a Spirit filled church in my hometown of Las Vegas, Nevada. A special speaker by the name of Mario Murillo and a worship leader Ron Kenoli were invited to come and hold a three day crusade at our church. During this time, I had not yet been exposed to a lot of teaching regarding the prophetic ministry. It was during these three nights of meetings that I encountered the reality of the manifest Presence of God with great anointing. I saw in action for the first time, detailed words of knowledge, healings, prophecy and powerful demonstrations of the Holy Spirit. As a newborn believer, I was in awe of the wonderful works of God. This prophetic encounter changed my life. This experience put such a hunger in my heart to know more of the Spirit of God and His gifts. By the grace of God I too have been used, by God, in releasing words of knowledge, healing, and prophecy. If God can use me, He can also use you to do the works of Jesus in the earth.

Since this experience, my family and I have had the privilege and opportunity to receive life changing impartations from my home church International Church of Las Vegas. It is an honor to be a part of a kingdom-size vision that is changing the spiritual landscape from Las Vegas to the nations around the world. The prophetic call of God on my life is to be His son, to hear His voice, and to be a voice in the wilderness crying out to the lost, the hurting, the broken, the destitute, and the depressed. There is forgiveness, hope, healing, and restoration in the heart of God for whosoever will come.

- GROUP DISCUSSION -

Read Luke 24:49, Acts 1:8, Acts 2:1-4,

1. Have you received the baptism of the Holy Spirit?

2. Do you speak in tongues? If not, do you desire to speak in tongues?

3. What is the purpose of the baptism of the Holy Spirit?

4. Are you fully yielded to the Holy Spirit?

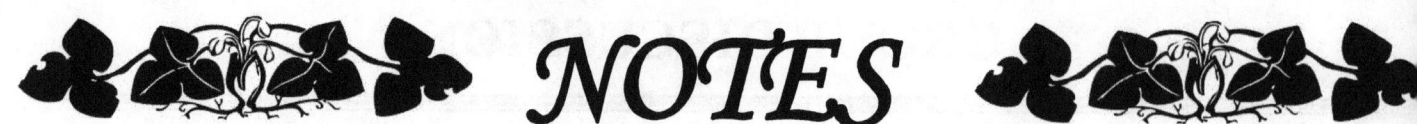

– ACTIVATION –

- ✓ Ask Jesus to baptize you with the Holy Spirit and expect to receive the awesome experience of the Holy Spirit baptism.

- ✓ Yield and surrender to the Holy Spirit by confessing your sins to God and your faults to one another.

- ✓ Position yourself to receive a Fresh infilling of the Spirit of God. Ask leaders in the church to pray with and for you to receive a fresh baptism of the Holy Spirit.

- ✓ Share your testimony of how you were filled with the Holy Spirit.

- ✓ Continue to journal what God is saying to you on a daily basis.

- LIFE APPLICATION -

The Holy Spirit filled life is something that you can walk in on a daily basis. Starting today, ask God to fill you with the Holy Spirit on a daily basis. Renounce every other spirit and simply welcome the breath of God to fill you and empower your life and the words of encouragement you share with others around you.

CHAPTER 3
HEARING THE VOICE OF GOD

So then faith **comes** *by hearing, and hearing by the word of God.* Romans 10:17

NOTES

➢ FOUNDATIONAL TRUTHS ABOUT HEARING THE VOICE OF GOD

1. **You can learn to hear the voice of God.**

    Faith is a key for unlocking your ability to hear the voice of God. As you begin to learn how to hear the voice of God you may respond in 6 different ways such as: "**I sense it**"; "**I see it**"; "**I hear it**"; "**I feel it**"; "**I know it**" or "**I believe it**". These 6 ways are connected with your spiritual senses as described in Hebrews 5:14. *But strong meat belongeth to them that are of full age, even those who by reason of use have their senses exercised to discern both good and evil.* It is by reason of use that you will begin to exercise your spiritual senses and as a result see the mighty works of God accomplished in and through your life. You don't have to say "Thus saith the Lord" to let people know that God is speaking. I believe that it is best to simply say it just as it is listed above. This is where divine wisdom, discretion, and training will help us to **decipher** what God is saying and how to **release** what God is saying.

    You will begin to recognize the voice of God in one or even in all these 6 different ways. I was transformed when I gave my life completely to Christ at a Christian concert in December of 1986. I heard the voice of God calling me to a life of complete surrender through a singer named Reba Rambo. Shortly after this salvation experience, I began to work in a boys' home called the Mizpah Boys Home. It was a home for troubled, abused, and fatherless youth between the ages of 7 to 17 years of age. I truly had an experience of a life time as I positioned myself in the Father's heart by helping the orphan's of our society.

    I was 20 years old and I had been saved only a few months, when God spoke to me and called me into full time ministry. He used a Christian movie called "Fury to Freedom" which was the life testimony of a man named Raul Reese. Towards the end of this movie, Raul's life dramatically changed after committing his life to Christ. The movie shows Raul reaching out and preaching the gospel to kids at his old high school.

    While watching this movie, God placed a burning desire in my heart to work with kids. God spoke to me, not in an audible voice, but through a movie and by placing within me that burning desire. About six months later, I was in full time ministry working with troubled youth. Now, more than 17 years later, I have had the opportunity to become like a father and mentor to hundreds of fatherless, abused, abandoned, and broken youth. I've also had the privilege of leading thousands of youth to Christ and have counseled hundreds of hurting families. Even as a baby in Christ, it was the voice of God that I learned to recognize and follow.

2. **You were created with the ability to hear the voice of God.**
   The Old and New Testament scriptures reveal God communicating with individuals who were in covenant relationship with Him, as well as with those who were not. When God created man, He created man in His own image. Both Adam and Eve had the ability to hear the sound of God only after He breathed into them the breath of life. Prior to God breathing into them, they were a body with no spirit or life. Once they received God's breath of life they were awakened to the voice of God, just as revealed in Genesis 3:8a; *And they heard the sound of the Lord God walking in the garden in the cool of the day.* The very life breath of God that allows you and I to live has also given us the ability to hear His voice. Even those that have no relationship with God can hear His voice so that mankind is without excuse on the Day of Judgment.

   God will do whatever it takes to communicate with people, even if it means using a donkey, as He did with a man named Balaam (Numbers 22:28). Take for example the radio; a radio has been manufactured with an ability called a "receiver" in order for it to pick up sound that is traveling in the airwaves. A radio has an antenna that helps the receiver to lock in on the sound waves, allowing it to transmit through the speakers. It is only a matter of adjusting our "spiritual radio dial", so that we can tune into the God station. Our vocal chords and our bodies will then be responsible to transmit the sound by word and deed.

3. **God speaks in many creative ways.**
   One of the common themes throughout the bible reveals God speaking to people. As you study the different ways that God has communicated to people, you will discover that He speaks in a variety of creative ways. Over the last 22 years I have discovered different ways God speaks to people. I've learned to hear by experience, my own mistakes, other prophetic ministers, and the study of the scriptures. Many times we have missed the speaking voice of God because we did not know or recognize the voice of God; we allowed doubt or our own intellect and reason to

interfere causing us to miss the sound of God. The following section outlines some of the most common ways to recognize the language of God and how He communicates with mankind.

4. **The different ways that God speaks.**

a) **The "Written" Word of God:** God will speak to us through the bible. "Logos" is the Greek word that describes the written word of God, including Christ Himself. The bible or the "Logos" is the final authority for how we are to live our lives on earth. This is where we, as humans, have been given the rights to live according to the principles, precepts, teachings, and commands of God. Personal Prophecy does not add, nor take away from the canon of scriptures. Many cults such as the Mormons or Jehovah Witnesses have added to scriptures and even have a different translation of the bible that denies the very deity of Christ. Any words of prophecy that are given must align with the Spirit and context of the written word of God called the Logos. Read John 1:1 & 14 and 2 Timothy 3:16.

b) **The "Spoken" Word of God:** God will speak to us by divine illumination of the scriptures. There is another Greek word found in the bible that describes the word of God as the "Rhema". This term has to do with the "spoken word of God". Rhema can be considered a "now" word from the written word of God. Have you ever been reading the bible and while you were reading the bible, the Holy Spirit illuminates a particular scripture verse or story to your heart and mind? You then realize that God is speaking to you through what you're reading in the bible concerning your personal life and or the situation that you or others are facing. That is the "Rhema" word of God. I remember a time of getting very sick, where I could not even get up from my bed. I was saved only a short while, but I felt that it was a spiritual attack and not just some type of flu symptom. As I turned my bible to Psalms 91, the Holy Spirit began to illuminate my mind that I needed to read, memorize and quote the whole Psalm 91. God was giving me a strategy to combat this attack. I was able to take the written word (Logos) of God and apply its truth as a spoken (Rhema) word of God for me personally. Read Romans 10:8, 17; Ephesians 6:7; 2 Corinthians 13:1.

c) **Dreams:** God will speak to us through dreams. Dreams are similar to visions. Dreams are given while a person is sleeping and visions are given while you are awake. God can give dreams to both the believer and the non-believer. The interpretation of the dream comes from the Lord. Dreams will be given as a result of the outpouring of the Holy Spirit. [17] *'And it shall come to pass in the last days, says God, That I will pour out of My Spirit on all flesh; Your sons and your daughters shall prophesy, Your young men shall see visions, Your old men shall dream dreams.* Acts 2:17

We must remember that not every dream that we have is from God, so we must discern the source. I would encourage you to place a pen and pad next to your bed at night and ask God to speak to you in dreams. Pay attention to the details such as colors, numbers, people, and how you felt during and after you had the dream. There are many biblical examples of God communicating to mankind through dreams in both and the Old and New Testament.

Those in the bible who received God dreams

Abimelech	(Genesis 20:3)
Laban	(Genesis 31:24)
Pharaoh	(Genesis 41:8)
Joseph	(Genesis 37:5)
Jacob	(Genesis 28:12)
Solomon	(1Kings 3:5)
Nebuchadnezzar	(Daniel 2:3)
Joseph	(Matthew 1:20)
The Wise Men	(Matthew 2:12)
Jeremiah	(Jeremiah 31:26)

d) **Visions:** Visions are one of the most common ways that God speaks to people. There are visions that are like a picture or snapshot that flashes in your mind. As we sanctify our imaginations with the word of truth, the more clarity of visions will be received. Another form of vision is called an "Open Vision". These types of visions are more than a "mental image". They are like an interactive 3D movie that plays right before your eyes. These types of visions include you as one of the "characters" in a God produced film. Open visions can be as brief as 30 seconds. Length is not as important as the strength of the message that God is speaking in this type of vision. Open visions were very common with prophets such as Ezekiel, Daniel, Jeremiah, Micah, Habakkuk, and Joel. The Apostle Paul, Peter, John, and others in the New Testament also experienced these types of visions. In the book of Acts, Peter went into a trance and was given an open vision which communicated to the Jewish believers that God was also accepting the Gentiles into covenant. *⁹ The next day, as they went on their journey and drew near the city, Peter went up on the housetop to pray, about the sixth hour. ¹⁰ Then he became very hungry and wanted to eat; but while they made ready, he fell into a **trance** and saw **heaven opened** and an object like a great sheet bound at the four corners, descending to him and let down to the earth. Acts 10:9-11*

e) **Gentle Thoughts:** Psalm 139: 17-18 describes the thoughts of God towards us as outnumbering the sands of the seashore. Can you imagine how many grains of sand are on the seashore? It would be too many to count. God is not greedy with His thoughts. He loves to share them with His people. As you become more aware of your thought life, you will be amazed how God uses this type of communication. Many times God gives us a thought and we simply ignore it, discount it as our own thought, or we may simply reason it away. Consider your mind like a chalkboard and ask God to give you divine thoughts and ideas. The Spirit of God will begin to write the very **thoughts of God** on the chalkboard of your mind. Keep guard over your mind from impure, negative, critical, or condemning thoughts. This is crucial in clearly recognizing the voice of God through our thoughts. Memorizing scripture is a great way of keeping the thoughts of God in your mind. Read Jeremiah 31:33; 2 Corinthians 10:4-5; and Philippians 4:8.

f) **A Still Small Voice:** We see in 1 Kings 19:11-13 that God communicated to the prophet Elijah when he was in the cave of despair. *Then He said, "Go out, and stand on the mountain before the LORD." And behold, the LORD passed by, and a great and strong wind tore into the mountains and broke the rocks in pieces before the LORD, but the LORD was not in the wind; and after the wind an earthquake, but the LORD was not in the earthquake; ¹² and after the earthquake a fire, but the LORD was not in the fire; and after the fire a **still small voice**. ¹³ So it was, when Elijah heard it, that he wrapped his face in his mantle and went out and stood in the entrance of the cave. Suddenly a voice came to him, and said, "What are you doing here, Elijah?"* I love this story and how it reveals the nature of God towards His prophets when they are in a time of weakness, confusion, or even depression. God does not communicate harshly with His people when they are at a low time in their life. The only time that I see Jesus speaking harshly was to the religious leaders who were stuck in their pride and old ways of thinking. It is the kindness of God that leads us to repentance. We must learn to be still from the busyness of life and even in our ministry, so that we can hear the gentle still small voice of God. If you are close to someone you don't need them to scream in your ear to hear them. Are you so close to God that if He whispered you would be able to hear it? John the Beloved understood what closeness was when he was able to lay his head on the chest of Jesus. Read John 21:20; Psalm 46:10; Psalm 4:4.

g) *The Audible Voice of God:* As a boy, Samuel heard the audible voice of God in 1 Samuel 3:8 and thought it was his mentor ⁸ *And the LORD called Samuel again the third time. So he arose and went to Eli, and said, "Here I am, for you did call me." Then Eli perceived that the LORD had called the boy.* Adam and Eve were able to hear the audible sound of God. The disciples heard the audible voice of God the Father through the sound of Jesus' voice and they heard the voice of the Father directly on other occasions, such as on the mount of Transfiguration. I personally have only heard the audible voice of God call my name probably less than 5 times since I gave my life to Christ 22 years ago. I do believe that I will hear His audible voice more as I continue to walk with Him; however, if I only listened to God through the means of His audible voice, I would probably not have accomplished a whole lot in my 22 years of serving Him. Because I learned that God's primary way for speaking to me has been through visions, I have been able to see a lot more accomplished in my life and ministry. Read Matthew 3:17; Matthew 17:5; & Psalm 29.

NOTES

h) **Holy Spirit's Voice:** Jesus taught the disciples that the Holy Spirit will be the one to speak to us about the very things that are in the heart of Jesus. *¹³ However, when He, the Spirit of truth, has come, He will guide you into all truth; for He will not speak on His own authority, but whatever He hears He will speak; and He will tell you things to come. ¹⁴ He will glorify Me, for He will take of what is Mine and declare it to you. John 16:13-14.* This is an awesome reality that leaves every believer without an excuse of thinking "I never hear God talk to me". This would simply be untrue and may be very close to insulting the Spirit of God, because the Holy Spirit is not mute. This is why learning the language of God is essential for hearing His voice more clearly and more often. Every believer in Christ has been given a deposit of the Spirit of God; therefore, He becomes the primary guide and leader of your life. We should not seek after signs to be led by God, but we should seek after the giver of signs. The more we learn to be led by the Spirit of God, the quicker we will mature, walk in freedom, and see the destiny of our life fulfilled. Read Galatians 5:8 & John 14:16-17.

i) **Prophets, Preachers, and Teachers of His Word:** Another way of God speaks into our lives are through prophets, preachers and teachers. Just as your body has many members so does the body of Christ. Each member needs one another in order for it to function at 100% capacity. Imagine if the legs say to the brain, "I don't need you to speak into my life!" You would have a body that goes absolutely nowhere in life. The same is true if we fail to recognize that God will use people in our lives such as prophets, pastors, Sunday school teachers, evangelists, and even our own children. It is biblical for you and I to go to church and expect God to speak to us through a pastor's sermon. He will also speak through a prophet's word of encouragement, a personal prophecy given by other gifted saints, or your spouse telling you "no honey, I don't feel good about you going into business with that certain individual". This is the power of the prophetic movement of God. The more we gain understanding and clarity of how God speaks, the more we will have the opportunity to walk in the perfect will of God, which is ultimately the best place to be in life. Read Romans 10:14-15; 1 Corinthians 14:3; & 1 Peter 4:11.

j) **Angelic Visitations:** God can also communicate His purposes in the lives of His people through angelic messengers. We can read biblical examples of God communicating his plans to individuals through messenger angels in both the Old and New Testament.

OLD TESTAMENT	NEW TESTAMENT
• *Abraham* • *Jacob* • *Moses* • *Joshua* • *Balaam* • *Gideon* • *Manoah* • *Elijah* • *Elisha* • *Daniel* • *Zechariah*	• *The Shepherds in the field* • *Zechariah* • *Mary* • *Joseph* • *Jesus* • *Peter* • *Cornelius* • *Paul* • *John* • *The 7 churches in Revelation*

k) **The Gifts of the Spirit:** The scriptures reveal in Romans 10:17 *So then faith comes by hearing, and hearing by the word of God.* Each of the gifts of the Spirit is connected with your ability to hear the voice of God. It is this ability of hearing what God is saying that will activate your faith to step out and do what He is telling you. As you step out in faith others will hear and see the voice of God in action. Those believers who have the gift of prophecy are able to be used by God to release personal words of encouragement, edification, and comfort. Jesus was anointed with the Holy Spirit and power, healing all those oppressed by the devil, for God was with Him. His life of setting the captives free was in itself a testimony of God's love towards the oppressed. The supernatural flow of the Spirit through His people will speak loud and clear of how much God loves and cares for people. *²⁵ Jesus answered them, "I told you, and you do not believe. The works that I do in My Father's name, they bear witness of Me. John 10:25 (NKJV)* Hearing the voice of God will help you to activate the gifts of the Spirit. This is a key to unlocking people's hearts to receive the love of God. Read Acts 10: 38; John 4:10-19; Mark 16:17-20.

l) **The Fruit of the Spirit:** There are nine fruits of the Spirit revealed in Galatians 5:22-23. *²² But the fruit of the Spirit is love, joy, peace, longsuffering, kindness, goodness, faithfulness, ²³ gentleness, self-control. Against such there is no law.* Jesus said that you will know false prophets by the fruit that is produced from their lives. The bad fruit that false prophets and ministers produce speak to others. An individual who has their trust and confidence in God will be like a tree that produces good fruit. When you see a believer who is full of the fruit of the Spirit, this will speak loud and clear that they are trusting in God. Walking in the perfect will of God will produce the nine fruits of the Spirit. We need to take time and inspect the fruit of our lives. The presence of the fruit of the Spirit helps us to recognize the voice of God's approval and to witness that we are in the will of God.

m) **Being Caught Up by the Holy Spirit:** Keep in mind, being caught up by the Holy Spirit is not the same as astral projection. Rather, this was an experience that the apostle Paul had in 2 Corinthians 12:2-4. *² I know a man in Christ who fourteen years ago--whether in the body I do not know, or whether out of the body I do not know, God knows--such a one was caught up to the **third heaven.** ³ And I know such a man--whether in the body or out of the body I do not know, God knows-- ⁴ how he was caught up into Paradise and heard inexpressible words, which it is not lawful for a man to utter.* In the book of Revelation, John was also caught up into the 3rd heavens. He was able to hear and see prophetic insights from God. Ezekiel also experienced similar instances, where he was also caught up by the Spirit and was given prophetic insight. Read John 4:1-2 and Ezekiel 3:12-14.

NOTES

n) **Body Impressions:** Many who operate in the healing ministry often gain words of knowledge through physical body impressions. I have been given body impressions in certain areas of my body and or my emotions when I have been ministering and or entered a room with other people around. As I felt these impressions I was able to minister more accurately with what God was revealing to me about those around me. For example, let's say you walk into a room where there are other people. Suddenly you start feeling an impression upon your elbow. You may feel a slight pain or even a "tingling" type feeling in your right elbow; however, before you walked into the room you had no types of these body sensations or physical impressions. This could be God giving you insight about another person needing healing in the right elbow. Faith and courage is required to step out and actually ask if anyone in the room has a problem with their right elbow. You will be amazed at how God speaks through these types of body impressions. I encourage you to pay attention to your own body and do a "Body Check" when you are around others or you enter a place where people are gathered. There are times when I am ministering, that I can feel warmth on my hands which helps me to know that a healing anointing is flowing at that moment. As I step out to pray for the sick the results are supernatural and people are healed. Discernment and wisdom will help you to stay balanced in this realm of hearing God's voice.

o) **The Artistic Voice of God:** One of the most profound ways that God is able to speak to us is through the "creative arts" such as; sculptures, pictures, paintings, poetry, pottery, plays, musicals, dramas, modern day parables, scripts, writing, and even theatre. You can see examples of how God would use prophets in the bible in very artistic and dramatic demonstrations, such as Ezekiel. *[1] "You also, son of man, take a clay tablet and lay it before you, and portray on it a city, Jerusalem. [2] Lay siege against it, build a siege wall against it, and heap up a mound against it; set camps against it also, and place battering rams against it all around. Ezekiel 4:1-2.* Ezekiel is instructed to draw a painting of what God was saying to the city. I love the saying, **"Pictures are worth a thousand words"** because it is true. God has creative ways of capturing the heart and mind of man. Prophetic words can also be dramatized by "acting out" the word of God. This is why drama, skits, and movies are a powerful tool in shaping the minds of society. A prophet named Agabas also delivered a prophecy through a live mini dramatization. *[10] And as we stayed many days, a certain prophet named Agabus came down from Judea. [11] When he had come to us, he took Paul's belt, bound his own hands and feet, and said, "Thus says the Holy Spirit, 'So shall the Jews at Jerusalem bind the man who owns this belt, and*

 # NOTES

deliver him into the hands of the Gentiles.' Acts 21:10-11. I believe that believer's in Christ must take the Media/Entertainment Mountain and begin to release God's word through this creative expression. Jesus was a master at utilizing modern day parables of the day to illustrate spiritual truths of the Father. Jesus utilized parables that were connected with the culture of His day in order to speak into their lives the very truths of the kingdom of God. If we are going to be His Voice to this generation, we must tap into God's creativity with the language of today's culture making it relevant to those watching and those listening. Poetry and songs are utilized to release a prophetic sound that can capture the very heart and emotions of an individual. One third of the Old Testament was written in this type of style such as Job, Psalms, Proverbs, Song of Solomon, Ecclesiastes, and even the writings of the prophets and in fragments of the historical books. I remember as a new believer without really having a lot of knowledge of how God speaks, I would write a lot of poetry. As I would write, it would come out as words of prophecy.

p) **God's instrumental voice:** The sound of music can be utilized as a means to hearing the voice of God. Samuel, Elijah, and Elisha connected with prophetic worship that included the sound of musical instruments. The sound of an instrument when played by an anointed musician can release the sound of God. This was illustrated in 2 Kings 3:15-16. *But now bring me a musician." Then it happened, when the musician played, that the hand of the lord come upon him. And he said, "Thus says the Lord;' Make this valley full of ditches'.* King David helped to usher in a new level of worship which included the sounds of instruments in what is known as the tabernacle of David. This tabernacle which was later constructed by his son Solomon was to include worship, intercession and music night and day. In 1 Chronicles 25:2-3 king David strategically places prophetically gifted musicians who had the ability to prophesy with their instruments. *Of the sons of Asaph: Zaccur, Joseph, Nethaniah, and Asharelah; the sons of Asaph were under the dirction of Asaph, who prophesied according to the order of the king. Of Jeduthun, the sons of Jeduthun: Gedaliah, Zeri, Jeshaiah, Shimei, Hashabiah, and Mattithia, six, under the direction of their father Jeduthun, who propheisied with a harp to give thanks and to praise the Lord.* This *is an* amazing revelation of experiencing the sound of God through instrumental worship. The devil understands the power of instrumental sounds, because he himself was created by God with instrumental sounds (Ezekiel 28:13-15). Lucifer prior to his fall was the lead worship angel in heaven. The instrumental sound that was given to him was meant to bring honor and worship to God. Lucifer was filled with pride which caused him to be kicked out of heaven. This "vacancy" place of worship in heaven has now been filled by someone most precious and loved by God. That someone is called the "Bride of Christ" also known as the church. You and I have been invited to take this position to release sounds of worship bringing glory, honor, and praise to the King of Kings and the Lord of Lords. *We must capture the prophetic sound of God through instruments.* Many times I will include music in my devotions which helps me to hear what God is saying to me. God is releasing anointed musicians in this day who are able to utilize their instruments to prophesy.

q) **The voice of God through His creation.** God is able to use the beauty of His creation to speak amazing revelation. We see the example of Abraham when God utilized the stars in the sky to illustrate His plan for his life. *Then He brought him outside and said, "Look now toward heaven, and count the stars if you are able to number them." And He said to him, "So shall your descendants be." And he believed in the Lord, and He accounted it to him for righteousness. Genesis 15:5-6.* Many people in astrology look to connect with the stars in order to receive information about the future, but they fail to connect with **the Creator of the stars**, for a true source of prophetic insight. Romans 1:20 reveals this truth. *For since the creation of the world His invisible attributes are clearly seen, being understood by the things that are made, even His eternal power and Godhead, so that they are without excuse.* All of creation was brought into existence by the power of His spoken word. Embedded within His creation are the very sound waves of His voice. Jesus said that the rocks would cry out if we don't praise Him. Creation echoes the very splendor of God's majesty throughout all of this world and the entire galaxy. God is awesome!

-GROUP DISCUSSION-

1. Out of all the creative ways that God can speak to us, what are your top 3 primary ways that God speaks to you?

2. Have you discovered other creative ways that God has spoken to you that were not mentioned in this chapter? If yes, explain how God spoke to you and can you give scriptural reference for how God spoke to you?

3. Can you share some of the artistic ways that God has spoken to you such as a poem, song, sculpture, drawing, or even a simple "doodle"?

- ACTIVATION -

- ✓ From your experience, describe the specific creative way that God spoke to you as discussed in this chapter?

- ✓ Take a moment in the class and begin to activate your faith for healing by asking God to begin to give you words of knowledge through body impressions. Take a few minutes as a class to simply be still and quiet. As you are doing this pay attention to your body, if you suddenly have an impression that was not there before you started this exercise step out by faith and share what body impression your feeling and the specific location. Now believe God for healing if it proves to be accurate and there is another individual in the room who has need for healing in that same area.

- ✓ Take a few minutes and write down what God is saying to you now. For this exercise activate your faith by taking a pen and write down what you believe or feel that God is saying to you right now.

- LIFE APPLICATION -

I would challenge you to increase your time in the following areas: individual and corporate intercession that is under church leadership and covering; study the word daily; make yourself accountable to church leadership; and walk in humility and obedience to what God is telling you.

CHAPTER 4
UNDERSTANDING PROPHECY

¹ Pursue love, and desire spiritual gifts, but especially that you may prophesy. ² For he who speaks in a tongue does not speak to men but to God, for no one understands him; however, in the spirit he speaks mysteries. ³ But he who prophesies speaks edification and exhortation and comfort to men. 1 Corinthians 14:1-3

 # NOTES

➤ FOUNDATIONAL TRUTHS ABOUT PROPHECY IN THE CHURCH

1. **The subject of prophecy and prophetic ministry is a biblical mandate.** Prophecy and the prophetic ministry is something that we must desire and pursue. The bible can be considered prophetically inspired by God. In today's society, many lives are under attack with negative words and words of condemnation. People in the church have experienced verbal abuse and even attacks of the devil. Prophecy is one of God's greatest weapons to counter attack these words of death. The gift of prophecy has the ability to bring the church encouragement, edification, and comfort. Read 1 Corinthians 14:1-5; Isaiah 50:4; Proverbs 18:21.

2. **Prophecy is meant for each one of us.** The basic meaning of prophecy is simply God communicating His thoughts, plans, and purposes to all of humanity. It is the privilege of His sons and daughters to be the oracles of God to others. The Bible can be considered a personal prophecy to all of mankind. Personal prophecy can be spoken verbally, demonstrated with actions, or written down. Looking at the major and minor prophets we see that they delivered God's message in these 3 ways. Read 1 Kings17:7-16; Ezekiel 4; Jeremiah 30:1-3.

3. **Personal prophecy is partial, conditional, and progressive.** Many who receive a personal prophecy must understand how to respond to the word given. Many times we place words given to us on the shelf and simply do nothing about it. Many words are then left dormant within the believer and never germinate to full maturity. Prophetic words are always partial. Many times we want to know what is going to happen from the beginning to the end of life. God will give you portions at a time. By giving us portions, this helps us to continue to walk by faith, try our faith, and grow our faith. Personal prophecies are also conditional. When we are given a personal prophecy, God requires us to cooperate with Him to see it come to pass. An example of this is found in 2 Chronicles 7:14. The promise of God was to bring healing to the land, but there was a conditional word given that said [14] *if My people who are called by My name will humble themselves, and pray and seek My face, and turn from their wicked ways, then I will hear from heaven, and will forgive their sin and heal their land.* God's condition for healing was for His people to do a specific action, such as humble themselves, pray, seek, and turn from their wicked

ways. Personal prophecy progresses over a lifetime. Abraham provides us with a great example of how a prophetic destiny unfolds over a lifetime. He was a prophet whom God considered His friend. Abraham was obedient to what God would reveal to him and by faith he earned the legacy of being our spiritual father, just as God said that he would be a father of many nations.

4. **The Holy Spirit is the very source of prophecy and true prophetic ministry.** It is important to know that biblical prophecy and prophetic ministry must be inspired by the Spirit of God.[20] *Above all, you must realize that no prophecy in Scripture ever came from the prophet's own understanding,* [21] *or from human initiative. No, those prophets were moved by the Holy Spirit, and they spoke from God. 2 Peter 1:20-21 (NLT)*[13] *However, when He, the Spirit of truth, has come, He will guide you into all truth; for He will not speak on His own* authority, *but whatever He hears He will speak; and He will tell you things to come. John 16:13*

Today, throughout the world, we are seeing an increased interest in the supernatural. The rise of psychics, fortune telling, channeling, astrology, and other demonic type practices are bombarding society more rapidly than ever before. These practices make up a multi-million dollar industry. This has given opportunity for the devil to bring a false source of "prophetic type" abilities, causing people to be led astray. I believe that there has been a void in the church concerning the activation of the true prophetic gifting of the Holy Spirit; however, this is changing as the true prophetic ministry increases within the church across the world. It is the believer that should be able to speak into a people's lives and help them to see God's destiny for his or her life. The Samaritan woman at the well received prophetic insight by Jesus. This woman was trying to fill the voids of her life with other things that could not satisfy her. Jesus was able to see and speak prophetically into this woman's life, which changed her destiny and the destiny of an entire city. Jesus is the perfect model for "prophetic evangelism." Read John 4: 1-14.

5. **The sources for "prophetically" inspired words and or actions.** One of the gifts of the Spirit is called "Discerning of Spirits". This gift gives the believer the ability to see the source of people's words, decisions, lifestyle, and actions. Discerning of spirits is not limited to only evil spirits. Discernment can also discern the leading of the Holy Spirit both on personal and corporate church level. Many times when I am

preaching, teaching, or leading a prayer meeting, it is my ability to discern the leading of the Holy Spirit on what He is doing, so that I can simply follow His footsteps which result in a fruitful time. I have found that the more time that I spend with Jesus in prayer and reading of the bible, it has helped me to be more sensitive to what God is doing and what He wants to do in my life on a daily basis. Caution must be observed as not to allow a spirit of suspicion to operate in disguise of discernment. Being suspicious of people does not promote a healthy atmosphere of love and encouragement. Discernment does not go around finding everyone's faults, nor is it accusatory, or suspicious of others. The four sources for our words and actions include:

- **The Holy Spirit:** The gift of prophecy is one of the gifts of the Holy Spirit (1 Corinthians 12:10, 1 Corinthians 14:1-5, and Romans 12:6). When the source of any prophetic word or act comes from the Holy Spirit there will be good fruit. There will usually be a manifestation of God's presence. I love to see people touched by the manifest Presence of God through prophetically inspired words. After giving hundreds of personal prophecies over the years I am amazed at the manifest Presence of God that people are able to feel when they receive words that are truly inspired by the Holy Spirit.

- **Our own mind or spirit:** Jeremiah had to confront prophets who were speaking from their own hearts in Jeremiah 14:14. *14 And the LORD said to me, "The prophets prophesy lies in My name. I have not sent them, commanded them, nor spoken to them; they prophesy to you a false vision, divination, a worthless thing, and the deceit of their heart.* Prophecy is speaking the heart, mind, and will of God, sharing His heart and intents, and not our own opinions. Words from our own mind, spirit or own carnality, dilute the power of God's "Rhema" words and have no real fruit. It becomes a form of Godliness with no real power to be demonstrated. It would not be wise to give prophetic words of the Lord when you are angry or you have any judgment or prejudice against that individual or church.

- **An evil spirit:** Words and actions inspired by evil spirits must be confronted and dealt with. It is possible for Christians to allow the source of their words or actions be motivated by an evil spirit without realizing it. Peter was rebuked by Jesus as Jesus recognized the source of Peter's words as demonic in Matthew 8:33. An evil spirit can actually be disguised as angels of light, bringing a distorted gospel that is contrary to the written word of God as found in 2 Corinthians 11:14. We must not be afraid to test the spirits (1 John 4:1-3).

- **Angels:** It is possible for angels to bring messages to mankind, such as the shepherds who heard angels announce the birth of the messiah (Luke 2:8-14). Mary and Joseph were given a message from the angel Gabriel in regards to the birth of Jesus Christ (Luke 1:28-38). There are many other accounts of the interaction of the angels of God in the life of God's people. The New Testament describes angels as ministering spirits. *¹⁴ Are they not all ministering spirits sent forth to minister for those who will inherit salvation? Hebrews 1:14.*

6. **Discerning the voice of God.** Many claim to hear the voice of God and yet it is not the voice of God but the deceptive voice of the enemy. The increase of mental health issues continues to be one of the biggest problems in today's society. From the very beginning of creation, it is the deceptive practice of the enemy that tries to get you and I to believe a lie (2 Corinthians 11:3). There are many different voices that you and I will listen to on a daily basis. These voices will try to invade the space of your mind by the way of evil thoughts, dreams, written words, words spoken out loud, television, internet, movies or even music. The enemy's job is to release sounds that will promote fear, anxiety, confusion and chaos. At this stage, the church is learning how to hear the loving sound of our Heavenly Father's voice, which is speaking to us every day, all day long and even at night when we are sleeping. It is the believer's responsibility to be the voice of God in the earth that releases a sound that will produce faith, hope, and love.

7. **There are three elements to prophecy.** When giving a prophetic word to individuals or in a group setting, it is important to understand that the 3 elements to the word of prophecy are revelation, interpretation and application.

- **REVELATION:** These are the things that God begins to show us such as dreams, visions, gentle visions ect... You are responsible for this part of insight. Once you receive the revelation, it will be up to you, with the help of the Holy Spirit, regarding what to do with what you have received. The wisdom of God helps you to know what to do with what is being shown to you. It may mean for you to pray for the situation, or it may be a word that you are to share with the individual. It also may be a word of warning that can be given to leadership. There are times that words are given out of season, but it's the grace of God that helps us to give words that are in season. Fasting, prayer, reading the word, training, living a life of holiness, and obedience, all help us to have clarity regarding what to do with what we are shown.

- **INTERPRETATION:** What is the meaning of the revelation that you are given? Jesus would tell parables such as the seed that fell on the four types of soil. He would then explain to the disciples what the parable meant. The interpretation of any revelation from God will be given by the Spirit of God. Just because you receive the revelation does not mean you have the interpretation. This is why it is important to work as a team. Be willing to share your revelation, even though you may not have the complete interpretation. There are times that you simply share the revelation and as you share, the individual receiving the word may get the interpretation. Many times we can receive clear revelation, but then we miss it at the interpretation level. This happens when we try to add our own thoughts or opinions. This is an area that we must continually develop through study, as well as practice. The more often you have a chance to interpret dreams and visions, with training and the help of the Holy Spirit, the more clarity you will have in the area of interpretation.

- **APPLICATION:** This is the part of prophecy that requires the individual who is receiving the revelation and or the interpretation to apply it to their life. I encourage you to include the wisdom and counsel of church leadership if you receive prophetic words that give direction such as moves, marriage, jobs, finances, or any type of major change.

8. **The gift of prophecy.** Besides the gift of love, prophecy is one of the most beneficial of all the gifts to operate in, because it focuses on building, edifying, and comforting people. This is one of the gifts that God uses to expand His kingdom purposes and plans in the earth. This is why prophets and prophecy are a vital part of God's building plans for the church. Paul exhorts the church of Corinth to pursue the gifts of the Spirit, but especially that they would prophesy. Paul, who considered himself a "master builder", had key insight and revelation of what true prophecy can produce in the lives of believers. When we think of prophecy, we sometimes think of future events or the ability to tell the future. Prophecy is connected with both the present and future. Prophecy is not a psychic type ability, but it is the ability to "fore tell"(**future**) and "forth tell" (**present**) what God is saying today. When true words of prophecy are given, they bring clarity concerning God's plans for an individual's life. The gift of prophecy is to hear from God and speak for Him, with words of encouragement and comfort. The gift of prophecy includes a "cluster" of other gifts of the Holy Spirit such as:

- **The Word of Knowledge:** These are specific facts, from the past or present, about the individual, such as a person's name, what the individual was thinking, birth date, where they live, what kind of car they drive, or name of a spouse, relatives, or friends. The word of knowledge is supernatural revelation and insight about the person's life that you otherwise have no way of knowing. Read John 4:16-19 and 1 Corinthians 14:24-25.

- **The Word of Wisdom:** This is divine insight into the specific plans and will of God for an individual's situation or life. It provides divine strategies of what to do and how to implement what God is saying in any given situation. The word of wisdom may not be as spectacular as the word of knowledge; however, the applied results can prove to be just as spectacular for that individual's situation. We can see how a word of wisdom works in 2 Chronicles 20:20-25 when God gave strategy on how to defeat invading armies. The wisdom for sending out the worship team instead of the fighting

 # NOTES

men seemed foolish in the natural, but when it's given by God it proves out in the end. As the people followed the wisdom of God they were successful in battle. A word of wisdom can be seen in Acts 27: 30-31. The sailors wanted to escape their sinking ship by way of lifeboats, which would have been a reasonable thing to do considering the ship was about to sink. However, the wisdom of God operating through Paul gave instruction of what to do. These men listened and as a result, no one lost their life.

- **Discerning of Spirits:** To discern something means to make a distinction between spirits, such as angels, human spirits, and the Holy Spirit. True discernment is able to identify the root motivation or intent of an individual or individuals. It is not being suspicious, but it is supernatural revelation into the spirit realm, seeing and perceiving what is really going on. It can mean the ability to recognize the anointing and Presence of God in a church gathering or in a counseling session. It has the ability to recognize the **pleasure** or **displeasure** of the Lord in any given situation.

9. **The manifest Presence of God will be present when giving a true prophetic word.** The Presence of God is one of the most important aspects of releasing any of the gifts of the Holy Spirit, especially the gift of prophecy. There are professional motivational speakers who can do a good job at motivating people just by their own ability and eloquence of speech. The difference between motivational speaking and true prophetic encouragement is the Presence of God. This is what distinguishes the natural motivation of man from the supernatural impartation of God's encouragement through the gift of prophecy. After prophesying to hundreds of individuals, I have had the privilege of consistently sensing the manifest Presence of God while speaking into the lives of precious people. Moses understood the importance of the Presence of God in His life. He made a bold statement that is something we can apply to our ability to prophesy into the life of the church: *[15] Then he said to Him, "If Your Presence does not go with us, do not bring us up from here. [16] For how then will it be known that Your people and I have found grace in Your sight, except You go with us? So we shall be separate, Your people and I, from all the people who are upon the face of the earth."* Exodus 33:15-16

NOTES

10. **Faith is the key that will unlock the storehouse of prophetic words and insights.** The subject of prophecy is always linked with faith or a deep trust in God. The scriptures enlighten us that we prophesy according to the measure of faith that is working in our life. *Having then gifts differing according to the grace that is given to us,* let us use them: *if prophecy,* let us prophesy *in proportion to our faith; Romans 12:6.* Our faith is something that we can grow and mature over a period of time with continued practice. Your ability to prophesy will grow as your faith grows. Individuals who are anxious to move into prophetic ministry, who step ahead of God and try to prophesy beyond his or her current level of faith, will prove to be in error.

Prophecy without real faith is dangerous and can prove to be harmful for others receiving the word and for the person giving the word. Some people can see and hear mature prophets like Cindy Jacobs, Dr. Chuck Pierce, or Dr. Bill Hamon give long, deep, and very accurate pin-pointed words of prophecy. In their zeal, without knowledge, they will attempt to imitate them by prophesying without the measure of faith. It is important to not compare yourselves with others who may prophesy longer and/or more accurately than you. You are in the developmental stage and as long as you are prophesying according to the measure of faith given to you personally, then God will take your seemingly little prophecy, and multiply above and beyond your own understanding. This is why the exercising of your faith on a daily basis will cause your ability to prophesy to go to deeper, to be more accurate and be expanded in your sphere of influence.

Four keys to activate your faith:

- **Knowledge** of the truth. Become a student and learner. As you begin to hear and learn the truth, faith will begin to arise within you. Faith comes by hearing and hearing from the word. *[16] But they have not all obeyed the gospel. For Isaiah says, "Lord, who has believed our report?" [17] So then faith comes by hearing, and hearing by the word of God. Romans 10:16-17.* It is the experiential knowledge of the truth that will bring freedom into your life so that you can free others.

- **Believe** that God will use you to do the supernatural. Can you truly believe and trust God to fill you with the Holy Spirit and manifest the gifts of the Spirit? Trust will give you access into the doorway of the power of His kingdom on earth as it is in heaven. *So Jesus answered and said to them, "Have faith in God. [23] For assuredly, I say to you, whoever says to this mountain, 'Be removed and be cast into the sea,' and does not doubt in his heart, but believes that those things he says will be done, he will have whatever he says. [24] Therefore I say to you, whatever things you ask when you pray, believe that you receive them, and you will have them. Mark 11:22-24*

- **Receive** from God and from those He uses to impart into your life. This is the power of impartation principal that Jesus gave to His disciples. *[1] Then He called His twelve disciples together and gave them power and authority over all demons, and to cure diseases. [2] He sent them to preach the kingdom of God and to heal the sick. Luke 9:1-2.* Paul also recognizes this truth as he himself was a carrier and an imparter of the gifts of God. *[11] For I long to see you, that I may impart to you some spiritual gift, so that you may be established-- Romans 1:11*

- **Be a doer** of what you believe. Unless you are willing to step out in faith and do something about it, your faith will be dead. Faith without works is dead. If you believe God to heal the sick, but never pray for the sick, then the reality of your faith would be considered dead. *[17] Thus also faith by itself, if it does not have works, is dead. James 2:17.* Being a "doer" of the word makes your life built on a solid foundation that will keep you strong in faith no matter what circumstance, struggle, or opposition comes upon your life. Jesus made this point clear in Matthew 7:24-27.

- GROUP DISCUSSION -

1. What are the qualifications for someone to prophesy?

2. Do you have the gift of faith operating in and through your life right now? Explain

3. Have you ever received words that were motivated by something other than God?

4. Have you ever had any experiences in the realm of psychic abilities such as astrology, hypnosis, astral projection, séance, palm readings, or fortune telling?

5. What was the motivation spirit behind these types of experiences?

6. Have you repented and renounced any and all associations with these types of practices? Break all past agreements and or association by word or deed from all works and practices of witchcraft and any other form of occult practices.

 NOTES

- ACTIVATION -

- ✓ Ask God to empower your life with a new measure of faith so that your ability to prophesy increases to a new level.

- ✓ Ask God to activate the gift of the word of knowledge, the gift of the word of wisdom and the discerning of spirits.

- ✓ Start by practicing words of knowledge within a small group setting of 3 to 4 individuals. Each take turns by asking God to give you a word of knowledge about thier life that you had no previous knowledge of. Take a moment to pray in the Spirit then quiet yourself before the Lord and expect a word of knowledge to be released to you. Step out and share what you have no matter how silly it may seem. Take turns so that each of you have a chance to practice.

- LIFE APPLICATION -

There are a multitude of individual prophecies stored in the heart and mind of God. Faith is the key for you to open the floodgates of prophecy that will flow to you and through you. Be willing to step out in faith by opening your heart and mouth and see how God will fill it with His words of life.

This key faith is being released to you; so receive a new measure of faith to prophesy into peoples' lives.

CHAPTER 5
SHARING THE VOICE OF GOD

[4] *"The Lord G*OD *has given me the tongue of the learned, that I should know how to speak a word in season to him who is weary. He awakens me morning by morning; He awakens my ear to hear as the learned.*
Isaiah 50:4

NOTES

➢ FOUNDATIONAL TRUTHS FOR SHARING GOD'S VOICE WITH OTHERS

1. **You were created to share His voice.**

   Like Ezekiel in the midst of the Valley of dry bones, God desires to release His breath of life through your words of prophecy. Ezekiel's anointing and calling as a prophet produced tangible fruit that was good. Ezekiel was able to receive the voice of God and to prophesy exactly what God was telling Him. The results of His prophecy were dead, dry bones transformed into an army of God full of the breath of God. The power of prophecy has the ability to change the present and future destinies of individuals and nations. You can share words of prophecy that can make a difference in those around you. *Also He said to me, "Prophesy to the breath, prophesy, son of man, and say to the breath, 'Thus says the Lord GOD: "Come from the four winds, O breath, and breathe on these slain, that they may live."'" So I prophesied as He commanded me, and breath came into them, and they lived, and stood upon their feet, an exceedingly great army. Ezekiel 37:9-10.*

   The prophet Samuel shared the voice of God with others and not one of the words from God fell to the ground. God was with Samuel and when He spoke everyone listened and received. *¹⁹ So Samuel grew, and the LORD was with him and let none of his words fall to the ground. 1 Samuel 3:19.* You and I will be given opportunities to share His voice with others around us on a daily basis. When was the last time you shared His voice with another person? Jesus prophesied in John 7:38 that rivers of living water would flow out from within their hearts. The prophetic ministry is not a "self-serving" ministry. The response of prophetic people should be like Isaiah who had a throne room encounter with God and cried out "here am I, send me!" *Then one of the seraphim flew to me, having in his hand a live coal which he had taken with the tongs from the altar. ⁷ And he touched my mouth with it, and said: "Behold, this has touched your lips; your iniquity is taken away, and your sin purged." ⁸ Also I heard the voice of the Lord, saying: "Whom shall I send, and who will go for Us?" Then I said, "Here am I! Send me." Isaiah 6:6-8.*

2. **You were created as a prophetic sign pointing others in the right direction.**
   ¹⁰ *"You are My witnesses," says the LORD, "And My servant whom I have chosen,*

That you may know and believe Me, And understand that I am He. Before Me there was no God formed, Nor shall there be after Me. Isaiah 43:10. As you study the lives of the prophets from both the Old and New Testament one of the common threads woven into their lives is their ability to hear God and their willingness to share what they heard with others. They themselves became a sign from God that He was trying to get their attention and turn His people back on the right path. *⁴ And the LORD has sent to you all His servants the prophets, rising early and sending them, but you have not listened nor inclined your ear to hear. Jeremiah 25:4.* The very nature of God is to reach out to His people who have gone astray or have been backslidden in their ways. The heart of God is for mankind to be reconciled back to Himself. The prophetic movement of God carries, within its very DNA, the ministry of reconciliation. Reconciling people back to God is the fruit of any prophetic ministry.

    a. <u>Prophets are not to be the center of attention for those around them; rather, they are meant to be a sign in the roadway of life that is pointing others in the right direction.</u> In Las Vegas, where I live, there are many colorful and creative signs that light up the city trying to entice people to come into the casinos or places of business. The signs that these establishments put up are meant to attract people's attention to their event, business, or establishment. God is very creative in the ways that He designs His prophets and His prophetic people. They will be a beautiful and inviting sign of His voice in the wilderness.

    b. <u>The prophetic ministry in itself carries very colorful expressions of anointing, miracle working power, supernatural signs, wonders, and healings. These colorful expressions are used by God to capture the attention of those who have gone astray from Him.</u> Jesus who is the Messiah and the greatest prophet is an example of His willingness to reach out to individuals in need of reconciliation. Jesus revealed the voice of the Father's heart to the lost and broken. This was seen in the account of the woman at the well. *¹³ Jesus answered and said to her, "Whoever drinks of this water will thirst again, ¹⁴ but whoever drinks of the water that I shall give him will never thirst. But the water that I shall give him will become in him a fountain of water springing up into everlasting life." ¹⁵ The woman said to Him, "Sir, give me this water, that I may not thirst, nor come here to draw." ¹⁶ Jesus said to her, "Go, call your husband, and come here." ¹⁷ The woman answered and said, "I have no husband." Jesus said to her, "You have well said, 'I have no husband,' ¹⁸ for you have had five husbands, and the one whom you now have is not your husband; in that you spoke truly." ¹⁹ The woman said to Him, "Sir, I perceive that You are a prophet. John 4:13-19.*

c. <u>Jesus' nature as a prophet gave Him insight into this woman's life that grabbed her attention.</u> This is such a great example of how prophets and prophetic ministry are supposed to utilize their call and gifting. Prophecy is not meant to build a big self-ministry or reputation. It is meant to build up people and bring the lost back to God the Father. We must be willing to take prophecy and the prophetic movement outside of the four walls and let the river of God flow into the mainstreams of everyday life around us. After being saved for about six months, I remember God's love compelling me to go and share His love with others outside of the church. I started by street witnessing on Friday nights right on the downtown streets of Las Vegas. This desire to "reach out" also led me into parks, prisons, the mission field of Mexico, and other nations of the world, where I am a sign for God pointing thousands of people towards Him. *¹⁸ Here am I and the children whom the LORD has given me! We are for **signs and wonders** in Israel From the LORD of hosts, Who dwells in Mount Zion. Isaiah 8:18.* As you begin to take prophecy and the prophetic ministry outside of the four walls of the church and let it be released in the world, the prophetic call on your life will shift to a new level.

3. **Your example and lifestyle can speak to others around you.**
Jesus explained clearly what it means to live life as foolish or live life as wise. *²⁴ "Therefore whoever hears these sayings of Mine, and does them, I will liken him to a wise man who built his house on the rock: ²⁵ and the rain descended, the floods came, and the winds blew and beat on that house; and it did not fall, for it was founded on the rock. ²⁶ But everyone who hears these sayings of Mine, and does not do them, will be like a foolish man who built his house on the sand: ²⁷ and the rain descended, the floods came, and the winds blew and beat on that house; and it fell. And great was its fall." Matthew 7:24-27.* Have you ever heard of the saying "Do as I say and not as I do"? Everyone who has a biblical knowledge and understanding

NOTES

would know that this is not a true statement. The life of every believer who claims to be a follower of Christ should be demonstrated not by word only, but by actions. The Apostle Paul wrote a statement to the church saying "follow me as I follow Christ".

   a. Paul's lifestyle became an example and standard that others could not only hear, but they could actually see demonstrated in real life. The religious leaders that Jesus confronted, could easily tell others what God was saying, but they themselves could not live it out. Many know how to "talk the talk" but have no idea of how to "walk the walk". This has "turned off" many nonbelievers because of the poor example of those claiming to be Christian.

   b. As believers in Christ, the scriptures admonish us the following command; *[23] And whatever you do, do it heartily, as to the Lord and not to men, [24] knowing that from the Lord you will receive the reward of the inheritance; for you serve the Lord Christ. [25] But he who does wrong will be repaid for what he has done, and there is no partiality. Colossians 3:23-25.* Many Christians, who are working in secular workplaces, have some of the greatest opportunities to be a mighty voice of God just by their work habits. If we are going to be a voice of God to others around you then we must first live the voice of God for others to hear loud and clear by our actions. *[16] By this we know love, because He laid down His life for us. And we also ought to lay down our lives for the brethren. [17] But whoever has this world's goods, and sees his brother in need, and shuts up his heart from him, how does the love of God abide in him? [18] My little children let us not love in word or in tongue, but in deed and in truth. 1 John 3:16-18.*

4. **You must receive boldness and courage to share the Voice of God.** *[17] "Therefore prepare yourself and arise, And speak to them all that I command you. Do not be dismayed before their faces, Lest I dismay you before them. [18] For behold, I have made you this day A fortified city and an iron pillar, And bronze walls against the whole land-- Against the kings of Judah, Against its princes, Against its priests, And against the people of the land. [19] They will fight against you, But they shall not prevail against you. For I am with you," says the LORD, "to deliver you." Jeremiah 1:17-19.*

a. The prophetic call of Jeremiah was not easy to fulfill. As a matter of fact, the life of a true believer in Christ is not a road of great ease. Jesus made it clear to His disciples that there would be great trouble and tribulation they would face all on the account of Him. Jesus made it clear to His disciples that there would be hard times, rejection, persecution, and even death. However, Jesus did promise them that He would be with them always, even unto the very ends of the world. This is where many prophets and prophetic ministries must endure as they desire to be the voice of God to their generation.

b. Ezekiel was given the responsibility to give warning to both the nation of Israel and to the wicked. If Ezekiel failed to say what God was telling him, then the blood of the people would be on his hands. As long as he spoke what God was telling him he would deliver his own soul from judgment. Many people want the title of "prophet" or "prophetic" yet they are not willing to count the cost of this type of calling. It can be very spectacular and awe inspiring, yet it also comes with much warfare.

c. The Apostles encountered resistance and persecution for being a voice for God in the book of Acts. *[18] So they called them and commanded them not to speak at all nor teach in the name of Jesus. [19] But Peter and John answered and said to them, "Whether it is right in the sight of God to listen to you more than to God, you judge. [20] For we cannot but speak the things which we have seen and heard." [21] So when they had further threatened them, they let them go, finding no way of punishing them, because of the people, since they all glorified God for what had been done. Acts 4:18-21.* The response to this type of resistance for prophets and the prophetic ministry is found in verse 20 and in Acts 4:23-31. They did not let fear and the intimidation of men stop them from sharing the voice of God.

5. **The corporate Prayer gathering.** The early church called for a corporate gathering of prayer where they were again empowered by the Holy Spirit, which gave them the courage and boldness to keep speaking the word of God to their generation. *²³ And being let go, they went to their own companions and reported all that the chief priests and elders had said to them. ²⁴ So when they heard that, they raised their voice to God with one accord and said: "Lord, You are God, who made heaven and earth and the sea, and all that is in them, ²⁵ who by the mouth of Your servant David have said:* 'Why did the nations rage, And the people plot vain things? ²⁶ The kings of the earth took their stand, And the rulers were gathered together Against the LORD and against His Christ.' ²⁷ "For truly against Your holy Servant Jesus, whom You anointed, both Herod and Pontius Pilate, with the Gentiles and the people of Israel, were gathered together ²⁸ to do whatever Your hand and Your purpose determined before to be done. ²⁹ Now, Lord, look on their threats, and grant to Your servants that with all boldness they may speak Your word, ³⁰ by stretching out Your hand to heal, and that signs and wonders may be done through the name of Your holy Servant Jesus." ³¹ And when they had prayed, the place where they were assembled together was shaken; and they were all filled with the Holy Spirit, and they spoke the word of God with boldness. Acts 4:23-31. This account becomes a great model for the persecution that is rising against the church in the time that we are living in right now. We can not shrink back and be silenced, but on the contrary, the voice of God becomes louder the more the devil tries to stop it.

NOTES

- GROUP DISCUSSION -

1. What are some of the obstacles that you must overcome when it comes to sharing His voice with others around you?

2. Are you willing to be used by God as His voice to others around you, from this day forward?

3. Are you willing to endure suffering, persecution, and rejection? Explain how you are going to deal with the fear of man.

NOTES

- ACTIVATION -

- ✓ Begin to prophecy your day when you get up in the morning. Instead of speaking words of death over your day begin to speak words of life.

- ✓ Name some specific people that you are praying for who need to hear the voice of God. Ask God to give you a word of encouragement for their lives.

- ✓ Begin to engage in prophetic evangelism also known as "treasure hunting" in the places that you go to during the week. You can do this by teaming up with another person or a small group. You can go on a "treasure hunt" searching for the diamonds of people's prophetic destiny that you can call out.

- ✓ Utilizing the gifts of the Spirit are great evangelism tools that will capture peoples' attention and their hearts, so begin to activate your faith by stepping out in faith sharing His voice with others.

- LIFE APPLICATION -

Jesus said that in this world we will encounter tribulation, but He said to be of good cheer because He has overcome the world. God has not give you a spirit of fear but a spirit of power, love, and sound mind. The same Spirit that resided in Christ while on this earth is now living in you; therefore, you can trust God and walk in the Peace of God no matter what trial or tribulation you may encounter.

CHAPTER 6
THE PROPHETIC MINISTRY

⁵ But one of the elders said to me, "Do not weep. Behold, the Lion of the tribe of Judah, the Root of David, has prevailed to open the scroll and to loose its seven seals." Rev 5:5

 # NOTES

➢ **FOUNDATIONAL TRUTHS THAT DESCRIBE PROPHETIC MINISTRY**

1. **Defining what "prophetic" ministry involves.** Below is a diagram to help clarify and interpret what prophetic ministry involves. The concept of prophetic ministry is inter-linked with multiple biblical truths. The use of the term "prophetic" includes everything described in the following diagram.

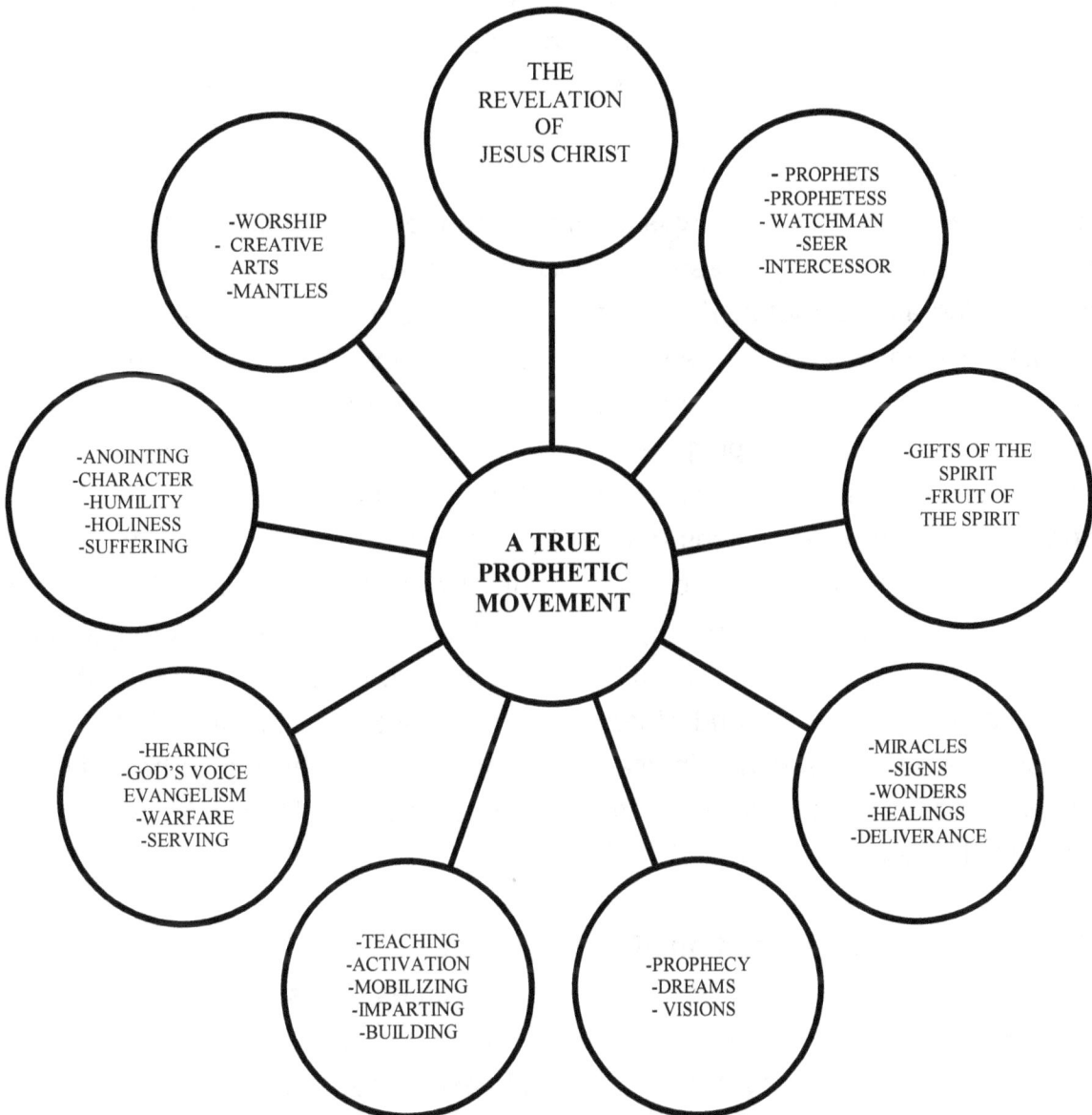

A. The word "prophetic" comes from the Greek word "Prophētikos". This word is described as pertaining to a foreteller of prophecy. It is also rooted in the Greek word "Prophētēs" which means foreteller, prophet, an inspired speaker or a poet.

2. **Understanding of the role of prophets within the church.** Recognizing the role of the prophets as one of the five-fold ascension ministry gift helps you gain clarity of their role in the body of Christ. There are many who would claim the title, but in actuality they are self-appointed and not appointed by God. Jesus had already prophesied that false prophets would arise in the last days. *[15] "Beware of false prophets, who come to you in sheep's clothing, but inwardly they are ravenous wolves.* Matt 7:15-17. The Apostle Paul gave caution to the elders of the church to keep watch over the flock. *[30] Also from among yourselves men will rise up, speaking perverse things, to draw away the disciples after themselves. Acts 20:30*

3. **True prophets will cause the heart of men to come into a closer relationship with Jesus.** Authentic humility is a primary mark of a true prophet. I remember one day while I was praying, I heard the voice of God asking me a question. He simply asked "Who are you Johnny?" I began to go through a list of "titles" thinking in my mind, "I'm a Pastor, teacher, evangelist, minister, ect." All of a sudden, I heard the Lord speak so clear in my mind saying "Johnny you are my son". At this point, I realized that God was helping me identify and clarify that my true identity in Him is not based on titles; rather, it is based on the concept of "sonship". To me, this was one of the greatest revelations that I've ever received from the Lord. Many people, in ministry and in the world, base their identity in what they do. True identity is based on who God the Father says you are. Many people are quick to take the title of "prophet" because of the lack of true identity. If you are a prophet then the fruit of your life will speak loud and clear. We should not seek the title, but we should always seek relationship and intimacy, as a son or daughter and co-heir with Christ. At Jesus' baptism, He was identified by The Father saying "This is My Son in whom I am well pleased." *Matthew 3:17*

4. **Prophets point to a revelation of Jesus Christ.**
   Prophets help to reveal the very nature and attributes of Jesus Christ. In the book of Revelation, John sees a new picture of Jesus as the Lion of the Tribe of Judah. In Revelation 19, John sees a new picture of Jesus as the rider on the white horse. This is the power of prophecy to help the church and the world see the resurrected Jesus as He truly is. I love this description of Jesus as the Lion of Judah. The lion is considered the "king of the jungle" and it is the roar of the lion that releases a sound of authority that is like no other. A few years ago, I remember going to the San Diego Zoo to visit the animals at the large open park area where they had all kinds of really cool jungle animals. In one area of the park there were male and female

lions. I had never seen a lion that close before and they were actually roaring. It was the first time I had ever heard a lion roar in real life. The sound that this lion made was as if there was a 1000 watt amplifier and a loud speaker inside its throat. It was amazing that such a deep sound could come out of an animal. As I sat there watching this huge cat, one of the trainers told a story of an incident that happened 5 years previous. The trainer said that there was a dairy farm just about 2 miles away from this location that was in business before they brought the lions into this current facility. When they brought the lions into the park the lions' roar was so loud and terrifying that all the cows on the dairy farm became sterile and stopped producing milk. The farm was closed down because of this.

This story spoke loud and clear to me as I began to relate this to the power of God's roar. When God releases His voice in the earth realm, through His prophets, it brings a terror into the camp of the enemy. The lies of the devil become sterile (void) by the revelation of God's voice of love to those held captive by its lies. Suddenly the devil's business of producing lies is shut down within the life of individuals, churches, territories, and the nations. When God touches your mouth with a prophetic call and anointing, you will walk in great potency of the roar of the Lion of the Tribe of Judah that brings terror to the devil and blessing to the children of God. *9 Then the LORD put forth His hand and touched my mouth, and the LORD said to me: "Behold, I have put My words in your mouth. 10 See, I have this day set you over the nations and over the kingdoms, To root out and to pull down, To destroy and to throw down, To build and to plant." Jeremiah 1:9-10*

5. **Prophets prepare the people.** You and I must be prepared and alert for the coming of the Lord in these the last of the last days. The prophet Isaiah and John the Baptist heard the voice of God personally and both understood their purpose in life. Likewise, we the church have been given the mandate to be a worshipper of God and the voice of God in the wilderness to our generation. *3 The voice of one crying in the wilderness: "Prepare the way of the LORD; Make straight in the desert A highway for our God. 4 Every valley shall be exalted And every mountain and hill brought low; The crooked places shall be made straight And the rough places smooth; 5 The glory of the LORD shall be revealed, And all flesh shall see it together; For the mouth of the LORD has spoken." Isaiah 40:3-5*

 # NOTES

6. **Prophets pave the way.** Prophets help to pave a way of holiness by leading a life of holiness and proclaiming the message of holiness. *[8] A highway shall be there, and a road, And it shall be called the Highway of Holiness. The unclean shall not pass over it, But it shall be for others. Whoever walks the road, although a fool, Shall not go astray. [9] No lion shall be there, Nor shall any ravenous beast go up on it; It shall not be found there. But the redeemed shall walk there, Isaiah 35:8-9.* The highway of Holiness is God's heart for the prophetic ministry. My friend Sergio Scataglini coins the term as the "100% Walk". Prophets help to pave this road with a lifestyle of prayer, obedience, true holiness, character, integrity, and skillful hands.

Prophets help to pave the highway of Holiness with "heavenly asphalt" such as seen below. As you run the race of faith, run with a heart to win.

```
                              ↓ LOVE
                        ↓ Repentance
                    ↓ Forgiveness
                  ↓ Fruit of the Spirit
                ↓ Gifts of the Spirit
              ↓ Anointing
            ↓ Prophecy
          ↓ Character
        ↓ Righteousness
      ↓ Suffering
    ↓ Truth
```
Wisdom

[1] Therefore we also, since we are surrounded by so great a cloud of witnesses, let us lay aside every weight, and the sin which so easily ensnares us, and let us run with endurance the race that is set before us, [2] looking unto Jesus, the author and finisher of our faith, who for the joy that was set before Him endured the cross, despising the shame, and has sat down at the right hand of the throne of God. Hebrews 12:1-2

- GROUP DISCUSSION -

1. Who are you? Explain in detail.

2. Explain what your idea of what a prophet is.

3. Have you experienced prophetic ministry from a prophet or prophetic ministry that was either improper, immature, or impure? Explain how you dealt with this.

4. Have you made the commitment to walk the 100% walk of holiness?

 # NOTES

- ACTIVATION -

- ✓ Begin to ask God for a fresh revelation of Jesus Christ for life and the life of the church.

- ✓ Ask God to anoint your eyes with spiritual eye salve so that you will have eyes to see what He is doing and ears to hear what He is saying.

- ✓ Humble yourself before the Lord and ask Him to give you the grace and gift of holiness to walk the 100% walk from this day forward.

- ✓ Repent and renounce any hidden sin or idolatry that would keep you from winning the race that is set before you.

- LIFE APPLICATION -

Make a choice today and determine today to walk 100% surrendered to the Lord from this day forward.

CHAPTER 7
RESTORATION OF THE PROPHETIC MINISTRY

[19] Repent therefore and be converted, that your sins may be blotted out, so that times of refreshing may come from the presence of the Lord, [20] and that He may send Jesus Christ, who was preached to you before, [21] whom heaven must receive until <u>the times of restoration of all things,</u> which God has spoken by the mouth of all His holy prophets since the world began. Acts 3:19-21

 # NOTES

➤ FOUNDATIONAL TRUTHS ABOUT RESTORATION

1. **The promise of restoration in the church.** Currently, there is a surge and a convergence of prophetic ministers, anointing, and training globally in the body of Christ. Jesus prophesied that His disciples would work as one, bringing glory to the Father by their love for one another.

   a. <u>Biblical History of the sons of the prophets.</u> Just prior to the birth of the prophet Samuel in the book of 1st Samuel, it was a time in Israel when the word of the Lord was rare and there was no open revelation. God's solution to this problem was the birthing of a Nazarite prophet named Samuel. The life of Samuel was birthed by the travailing intercession of a woman named Hannah. The name "Samuel" actually means "heard of God". We know that God hears and that God answers us when we call on Him. It was Samuel who initiated and established one of the first schools for gathering and training a company of prophets in Israel. Read 1 Samuel 10:5-13.

   b. <u>The birthing of a prophetic movement for this generation and beyond.</u> Since the 1980's there has been a major restoration and global movement in the realm of prophetic ministry. Before this time there was not a lot of teaching, training, and activation globally about the prophetic ministry. The benefits that the saints receive from the ministry of true prophets are the ability to operate in greater clarity of hearing the Lord's word, open visions, personal prophecy, intercession, strategic counsel, prophetic worship, spiritual warfare, and a greater intimacy with God.

   c. <u>Removing the veil of unbelief.</u> There are many church leaders across this nation that do not believe or have the knowledge of a "present truth" restoration of the prophets or prophetic movement. The plan of the enemy is to keep the leadership and the saints blinded to one of the most powerful weapons of spiritual warfare that God has given the church. The prophets' anointing has the ability to root out hidden strong holds, as well as confront principalities and spiritual wickedness in high places that hold individuals, families, and territories captive to their evil purposes. The prophet Jeremiah was God's weapon of choice for breaking the deceptive forces of false prophets, rebellion and idolatry that God's people had fallen prey to.

2. **The office of the Prophet is a vital role in the body of Christ.** The purpose of prophets is to equip, activate, and mobilize the saints into their membership ministry. In Ephesians 4:11 the scriptures reveal five ministry extensions of Christ Himself and what their roles are. Like the five fingers on the hand of a man, they each have there own specific function. as the five ministry extensions are:

- Apostles
- Prophets
- Evangelists
- Pastors
- Teachers

The five fold ministry is the hand of God that helps to equip, build and care for His people.

Chris Valloton writes about the five fold ministries as being the governmental offices in the church in *Basic Training for Prophetic Ministry (pages 22-23):*

Apostles govern. Apostles are similar to the general contractor who oversees the project and sees the overall picture.

Prophets guide. Prophets are the architects who assist the general contactor to know what the project should look like.

Evangelists gather. Evangelists' concern is for the lost.

Pastors guard. A pastor's heart is for the saved.

Teachers ground. A teacher's primary role is to help the flock understand the word of God.

3. **The church foundation involves apostles and prophets.**

    The two main ascension gifts, seen in Ephesians 4:11 are the offices of the apostles and prophets. Many believe or have carried the tradition that these types of gifts are no longer needed and there is no more need for the gifts of the Spirit. This is beginning to change, as there is the formation of new wineskin in many of the church leaders. They are becoming more open to the ministry and gifts of true Apostles and Prophets. There have been major restorative movements over the last 500 years of the church's history bringing back biblical and "present truth" revelation. One example of a global restoration movement of biblical truth includes the well known Pentecostal movement of the early 1900's. This historical movement that started in a small house on Bonnie Brae street in Los Angeles, California in 1906 with a man named William Seymour who himself had experienced the baptism of the Holy Spirit with the evidence of speaking in tongues. This man was a match, lit up with the fire of God. God used this man's life to spark a global restoration movement of the baptism of the Holy Spirit, gifts of the Spirit, and speaking in tongues. From this movement in 1914 there was the birth of the first General Assemblies of God that has since expanded into one of the fastest growing networks of churches all over the world.

4. **A movement of apostolic, prophetic and the saints on the rise.**

    Beginning in the early 1980's, there began a global restorational movement concerning the office of the Apostle and Prophet due to the labor of many prophetic and Apostolic forerunners such as Bishop Bill Hamon, Rick Joyner, Bob Jones, Dr. Chuck Pierce, Peter Wagner, Cindy Jacobs, James Goll, John Paul Jackson, Lou Engle, Mike Bickle, and other known and unknown Prophets and Apostles. These men and woman have helped to pave the way for the restoration movement of the office of the prophet and the apostle.

    The two offices of Apostle and Prophet are actually a part of the foundation of the church with Jesus Christ as the cornerstone. *[19] Now, therefore, you are no longer strangers and foreigners, but fellow citizens with the saints and members of the household of God, [20] **having been built on the foundation of the apostles and prophets, Jesus Christ Himself being the chief cornerstone,** [21] in whom the whole building, being joined together, grows into a holy temple in the Lord, [22] in whom you also are being built together for a dwelling place of God in the Spirit. Ephesians 2:19-22*

 # NOTES

We are now seeing the saints of God being activated and mobilized within their families, work environments, and places of influence, with great love and powerful signs, wonders, and miracle healings. Bishop Bill Hamon recognizes this as "the Saints Movement." The saints are arising with Holy Spirit momentum for the new millennium and are doing "greater works" that Jesus prophesied to His disciples in John 14:12:[2] *"Most assuredly, I say to you, he who believes in Me, the works that I do he will do also; and greater works than these he will do, because I go to My Father. John 14:12.*

What I See Coming In This New Millennium

- I see the five fold ministries, across the globe, coming together in a convergence of love and unity of the Spirit like we have not seen since the formation of the church in the book of Acts.

- I also see the mobilization and activation of the saints of God as the church and as the voice of God, the hands of God, the feet of God, and the heart of God to their families, neighbors, work places, their cities and the nations.

- The seven mountains of the kingdoms of this world are being invaded by both the five fold ministers and the saints of God. The revelation of the seven mountains that God desires to invade include:

    The Church
    The Family
    Education
    Business/Market Place
    Arts/Entertainment
    Media
    Government

- 2009 and beyond. The number 9 represents new birthing and a new wine skin: I say that there is the birthing of a global reformation movement that I term as the "Jesus Reformation". There will be a double portion of the revivalists, but there will be reformers who will bring reformation of the very mind molders of society. We must not allow an anti-Christ spirit influence our lives and the lives of our children? I prophesy that it's time for the Mind of Christ to be the influencer of America and the nations of this world.

- A global harvest movement of God is being released and the "angels of harvest" are being dispatched by the Father to be stationed and work alongside the churches that are obedient to the commander and Chief. *^{35} Do you not say, 'There are still four months and then comes the harvest'? Behold, I say to you, lift up your eyes and look at the fields, for they are already white for harvest! John 4:35-36*

- GROUP DISCUSSION -

Read Ephesians 4: 4:10-16, 1Corinthians 12:28 & Ephesians 2:20-22

1. What is the main purpose of the five fold ministry?

2. Do you consider yourself activated as one of the five fold minister or do you consider yourself an active member of the saints that is being mobilized to do the works of God?

3. In what ways do you see a work of restoration in your personal life, relationships, finances, family, or in the church?

4. Are you willing to be like Hannah, in 1 Samuel, who was able to give birth to a prophetic movement through her desperation, travail, and intercession?

 # NOTES

- ACTIVATION -

- ✓ Begin to engage in a deeper level personal prayer and include fasting. Isaiah 58 helps to describe the fast of the Lord that reveals specific breakthrough for your life both individually and corporately as the body of Christ.

- ✓ Begin to commit to at least once a week corporate intercession with in the local church setting under the approval of church leadership.

- ✓ Begin to expect any bareness in your life and the life of the church to be broken. (Barrenness means infertile or ineffective)

- ✓ Expect for great fruitfulness to be released as you begin to travail in intercession for the purposes of God and for sons and daughters to be birthed throughout the earth.

- ✓ Take time with the agreement of others in the class and ask God to release an anointing for you to operate in prophetic intercession, birthing the purposes of God through prayer and fasting.

- LIFE APPLICATION -

Expect the Spirit of God to bring you into the "birthing room" during these times of prayer and fasting. Through His people the restoration movement of the fivefold ministry and the saints will produce the greatest harvest of souls that this world has ever seen. Will you lay down your life in prayer to see this happen in our generation?

CHAPTER 8
EZEKIEL'S PROPHETIC RIVER

There is a river whose streams shall make glad the city of God, The holy place of the tabernacle of the Most High. Psalms 46:4

 # NOTES

Ezekiel's River

¹ Then he brought me back to the door of the temple; and there was water, flowing from under the threshold of the temple toward the east, for the front of the temple faced east; the water was flowing from under the right side of the temple, south of the altar. ² He brought me out by way of the north gate, and led me around on the outside to the outer gateway that faces east; and there was water, running out on the right side. ³ And when the man went out to the east with the line in his hand, he measured one thousand cubits, and he brought me through the waters; the water came up to my ankles. ⁴ Again he measured one thousand and brought me through the waters; the water came up to my knees. Again he measured one thousand and brought me through; the water came up to my waist. ⁵ Again he measured one thousand, and it was a river that I could not cross; for the water was too deep, water in which one must swim, a river that could not be crossed. ⁶ He said to me, "Son of man, have you seen this?" Then he brought me and returned me to the bank of the river. ⁷ When I returned, there, along the bank of the river, were very many trees on one side and the other. ⁸ Then he said to me: "This water flows toward the eastern region, goes down into the valley, and enters the sea. When it reaches the sea, its waters are healed. ⁹ And it shall be that every

living thing that moves, wherever the rivers go, will live. There will be a very great multitude of fish, because these waters go there; for they will be healed, and everything will live wherever the river goes. ¹⁰ It shall be that fishermen will stand by it from En Gedi to En Eglaim; they will be places for spreading their nets. Their fish will be of the same kinds as the fish of the Great Sea, exceedingly many. ¹¹ But its swamps and marshes will not be healed; they will be given over to salt.

¹² Along the bank of the river, on this side and that, will grow all kinds of trees used for food; their leaves will not wither, and their fruit will not fail. They will bear fruit every month, because their water flows from the sanctuary. Their fruit will be for food, and their leaves for medicine."
Ezekiel 47:1-12

> **Foundational truths about the 4 levels of the prophetic river of God**

   1. **There are fresh, life-giving waters flowing.** These are the greatest days for the church around the world to experience the prophetic river of God. It is the responsibility of every believer, church ministry, and church leader to press into new levels of the river of God. The prophet Ezekiel encountered the river of God that started at his ankles. The more that he moved forward in the river the more the water began to rise. It arose from his ankles to his knees, then to his waist until he could no longer walk because the water had risen over his head. If you are willing to press forward in this river with a desire to learn, understand and grow in the prophetic, you will find yourself swimming in these waters and you will prophecy like you never imagined possible.

The following is a diagram to illustrate the 4 levels of the prophetic river of God that is flowing globally within the local church. Like wading into a pool you can see that the further you step forward into this 'prophetic' pool, the deeper the waters become. I encourage you to simply jump into this life changing experience and allow the waters of Holy Spirit to overflow in and through your life, your family, and for the sake of Christ.

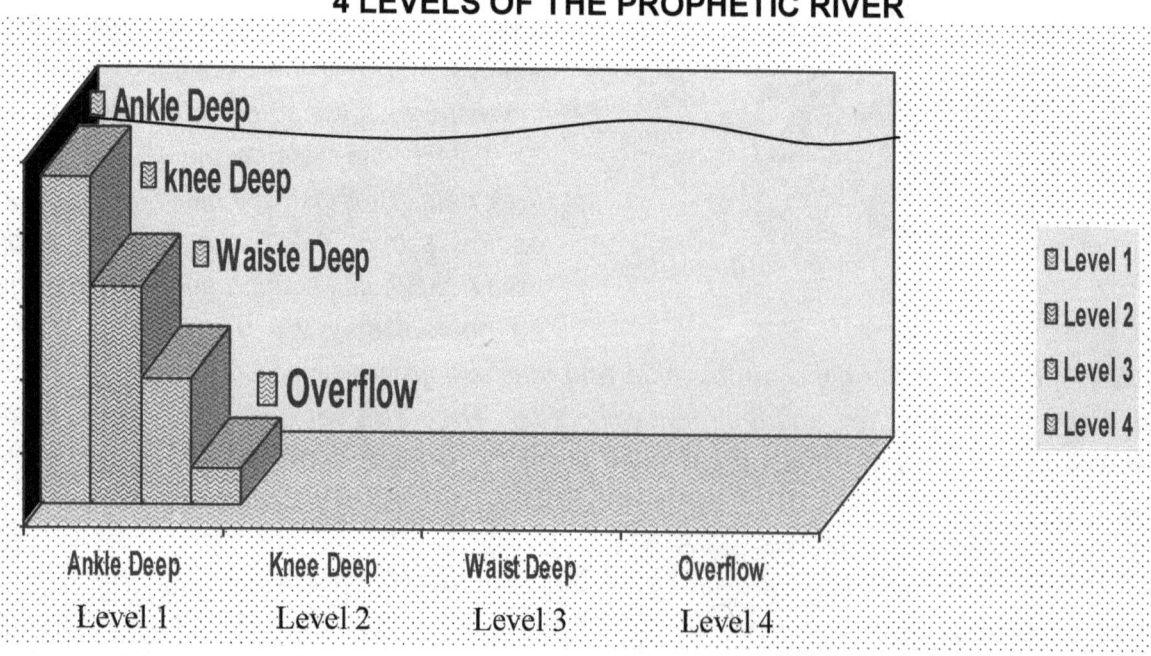

➢ FOUR PROPHETIC LEVELS DEFINED WITHIN THE CHURCH SETTING

Level 1- The Spirit of prophecy that releases a Prophetic Culture: Those who come into this type of prophetic culture will suddenly find themselves feeling accepted and loved by our heavenly Father. Many who have never had visions, dreams, and words of prophecy will find themselves experiencing these types of encounters with God. King Saul encountered a "prophetic culture" when he found himself among a group of prophets. He began to prophesy just like the prophets even though he had never done this before. *⁹ So it was, when he had turned his back to go from Samuel, that God gave him another heart; and all those signs came to pass that day. ¹⁰ When they came there to the hill, there was a group of prophets to meet him; then the Spirit of God came upon him, and he prophesied among them. ¹¹ And it happened, when all who knew him formerly saw that he indeed prophesied among the prophets, that the people said to one another, "What is this that has come upon the son of Kish? Is Saul also among the prophets? 1 Sam 10:9-11.* The secrets of hearts will also be revealed in this type of prophetic culture.

This term "prophetic culture" is used to help clarify and bring understanding of prophetic ministry within the church. These are churches whose leadership and shepherds accept, validate and desire the prophetic ministry. The "fear factor" concerning the prophetic ministry, as being something weird or even demonic, is confronted and overcome by the love of God, biblical training, and by healthy church leadership.

Training and accountability is a vital part for churches who desire prophetic ministry within their ministry. In this type of atmosphere the saints are encouraged, trained and activated in hearing His voice as well as sharing His voice with others. <u>A prophetic culture provides an atmosphere of humility and love, honoring one another as heirs and co-heirs with Jesus Christ.</u> There is usually at least one, and sometimes several true prophets who function within the church leadership. Within a prophetic culture there will be a desire for intimacy with God and love for one another. Jesus' desire for His church is for His house to be a house of prayer for all nations.

NOTES

The prophetic culture facilitates and develops the saints into corporate intercession. Intercession in the church is not just the responsibility of a faithful few, but each member of the body is challenged to be engaged in intercessory prayer in the local church. The church leadership who believe in and actively pursue prophetic ministry within their church will be benefited with the following:

- Saints hearing the voice of God
- Open heavens
- Visions
- Dreams
- Church members mobilized into ministry
- Prophetic pictures, poetry
- Angelic visitations
- Intimacy with Jesus
- Love for one another
- New songs and sounds in music
- Deeper experience in worship
- Intercession
- Signs, wonders, and healing
- Giving and prosperity in the church

Level 2-Gift of Prophecy: This level of the prophetic involves the saints receiving the gift of prophecy and they begin to operate in the revelatory gifts of the Holy Spirit found in 1 Corinthians 12:10, 14:1-5, & Romans 12:6. The gift of prophecy is being released in the church setting under the accountability of church leadership. The saints are being encouraged to prophesy in settings outside of the church such as their families, work place, in grocery stores, when they go out to eat, or wherever they go. At this level, those who actually have the gift of prophecy are now activated and under the training of mentors and church leadership. They are given opportunity to release words of God both individually and in a group setting.

The prophetic or revelatory gifts include the gift of prophecy, discerning of spirits, word of knowledge, and word of wisdom. At this level, individual saints within the church body are receiving and releasing personal prophecies for individuals who may attend the church and or they are releasing personal prophecies outside of the church with good fruit. The prophetic gifting is also being activated within all areas of the ministry,

NOTES

including the youth and children's ministry. Individuals are now being released by the leadership to give personal or corporate prophecies within the local church body and or ministry. These individuals have the gift of prophecy and can operate under the anointing of the Holy Spirit and with the Father's love and compassion.

[1] Pursue love, and desire spiritual gifts, but especially that you may prophesy. [2] For he who speaks in a tongue does not speak to men but to God, for no one understands him; however, in the spirit he speaks mysteries. [3] But he who prophesies speaks edification and exhortation and comfort to men. 1 Corinthians 14:1-3. Allowing the operation and the manifestation of these revelatory gifts within the church setting will result in much fruit and fruitfulness such as:

- Church unity and love
- The Joy of hearing His Voice
- A Deeper trust
- Peace of mind knowing God's will in the situation
- Boldness and courage to encourage others
- Confirmation and witness of what God is revealing to others
- Exercising the gifts of the Spirit
- Builders of the kingdom
- Edification in the ministry
- Exhortation of God's love
- Comfort and strength to the body
- The "Awe" of God's Presence

Level 3- The prophetic ministry, anointing and mantle: Ministries operating at this level will be developing and multiplying students, mentors, and teachers who can impart into the schools of prophets and prophetic ministry. At this level there is the developing of curriculum and teachings that help develop those called to the prophetic ministry. Individuals walking at this level will receive, carry, and serve with a prophetic mantle. Many who serve at this level of prophetic gifting are also called to the office of the prophet. Those who serve at this capacity continue to serve under the protocol of the house and it's ordained leadership. These individuals are able to release personal prophecy with accuracy, proven character, anointing and humility. Their proven fruit is evident of their love for God and people. Elijah mentored and trained Elisha who served faithfully for years. Elisha was able to carry on the mantle and prophetic legacy of Elijah the prophet and received a double portion of this prophet's heart and ministry. Because Elisha was truthful, submitted, and committed to God's ordained leader, he certainly reaped the rewards of "double portion". This is a great example of those walking at this level of prophetic ministry.

Level 4- A company of prophets: This is one of the five-fold gifting of Christ Himself. This is the ascension gift of Jesus the Prophet in the church. True prophets do not just function under the gift of prophecy, but they function from the five fold ascension gifts of Christ Himself. Prophets are the gifts to the church. They function in levels of authority as governmental leadership in the church, which gives him or her responsibility to equip, mobilize, and activate saints into the body for ministry.

Prophets will now bring direction, correction, and church discipline, as well as continued encouragement, edification, and comfort to the saints of God. Prophets also operate as watchmen on the wall, ready to warn of coming destruction of enemy invaders who attempt to thwart the work of God. They are releasing kingdom strategies for the church to be expanded in the earth. There are Prophets who have been called to pastor churches, so this would qualify the pastor to also function in the office of a prophet. Jeremiah is an example of a pastoral prophet calling. The best example is Jesus Christ who is the chief Shepherd and the Prophet of all prophets. Prophets are seen as those called to prepare the way of the Lord's second coming and prepare and purify the bride of Christ. They are special friends, close to the heart of God. God does nothing in the earth without first revealing to His prophets. Prophets and the saints are the apple of His eye and He gives admonishment to do His prophets no harm.

Prophets are usually called at birth or when they are born again. They must endure suffering, persecution, and even rejection just as Jesus said *[22] What blessings await you when people hate you and exclude you and mock you and curse you as evil because you follow the Son of Man.[23] When that happens, be happy! Yes, leap for joy! For a great reward awaits you in heaven. And remember, their ancestors treated the ancient prophets that same way. Luke 6:22-23 (NLT)*

Let the river flow

The river of God continues to flow from His throne and within the church. The river must not be contained in the 4 walls of the church. This prophetic river must be released into the world. You carry within you this life giving river that Jesus said would

 # NOTES

flow out of your inner most being. As God's chosen vessels we must continue to serve and honor the Lord in all that we say and do. God is drawing his people into new levels of the river that is resulting in one of the greatest outpouring of the Spirit of God that we have ever seen. Atmospheres are being transformed as the prophets declare the word of the Lord through out the whole world. In the book of Revelation 19:10 John is admonished to worship God. Jesus must receive all the glory and all the praise for it is the testimony of Jesus that is the Sprit of prophecy. It is by these testimonies that we will overcome just as Jesus overcame every evil foe and is now seated at the right hand of God. *"To him who overcomes I will grant to sit with Me on My throne, as I also overcame and sat down with My Father on His throne. He who has an ear, let him hear what the Spirit says to the churches".* Revelation 3:21-22

- GROUP DISCUSSION -

1) According to the 4 levels that are described in this chapter, what level of the river do you see yourself in at this moment?

2) Is your life progressing forward in the prophetic or has it gone backwards?

3) Is there a deep passion and desire to prophecy?

4) Does your church and or church pastor and leadership allow for prophetic ministry?

5) Have you ever given a word that you believed was God and church leadership did not respond to it the way you expected? How did you react and handle it?

 # NOTES

- ACTIVATION -

- ✓ Share a vision and or dreams that you believe that God has given you in class. After sharing the vision or dream, then pray as a group and ask God to give an interpretation.

- ✓ Wait upon the Lord and remember, it is not an "opinion" that you are looking for, it is an interpretation of what God is saying.

- ✓ Begin to step out in faith writing down prophetic words that you believe God is giving to you and share it with the church leadership.

- ✓ This takes courage and maturity on your part knowing that you have done your part and it is the leadership's responsibility to do their part.

- LIFE APPLICATION -

As you press forward in the prophetic river of God, your life will become a prophetic voice of God to the church that you are involved with. It is imperative that you stay connected and under covering of the church that you attend. You must be careful not to be a "lone ranger" and allow pride to disconnect your life from being under proper authority and alignment with the church leadership. This requires humility, a teachable spirit, and the grace of God. Keep pressing forward in the river of God and experience all that He has destined for your life.

CHAPTER 9
THE LANGUAGE OF GOD'S HEART

And now abide faith, hope, love, these three; but the greatest of these is love. 1 Corinthians 13:13

NOTES

➤ FOUNDATIONAL TRUTHS ABOUT GOD'S LOVE

1. **Love is the language of God's heart.** God's purpose for redeeming humanity is based on LOVE. John 3:16 reveals the whole reason for Jesus Christ coming to this earth. It was all based in God's love for the whole world. *For God so loved the world that He gave His only begotten Son, that whoever believes in Him should not perish but have everlasting life. John 3:16.* Recently, the Lord said to me "Johnny, increase your circle of love". As I pondered on this, I thought of Pastor Tommy Barnett who is one of the greatest examples for loving people, no matter who they are. I remember when Pastor Tommy came to ICLV several years ago and he said something that has stuck in my mind and heart ever since. In his message, Pastor Tommy talked about enlarging our circle of love, to include as many people as you can, regardless of who they are. Here is a man who can easily settle for ministry success in his church at Phoenix First Assembly; however, he chose to increase his circle of love to include other nations and cities such as the building of the L.A. Dream Center. He turned the old Los Angeles hospital into an inner city "spiritual" hospital of hope for the homeless, drug addicts, prostitutes, gang members, the fatherless, and the outcasts of society. Remember, God's circle of love covers the whole world.

   I realized that the Holy Spirit was prompting me to expand my circle of love to include more than myself, my family, my church or even my city. Allow the love of God to expand your circle of love to include even other nations. John who titled himself "the one whom Jesus loved" shows us the place of love that we must position ourselves if we are going to hear His voice. We must find ourselves laying our heads on his chest daily so that we can hear the very sound of the heartbeat of God that says loud and clear this is my son or this is my daughter in whom I love and am well pleased. Jesus, the greatest prophet himself, heard the voice of the Father affirming His love for Him: *17 And suddenly a voice came from heaven, saying, "This is My beloved Son, in whom I am well pleased." Matthew 3:17.*

2. **Love must be the motivation for any prophetic movement.** The church of Laodicea in the book of Revelation Chapter 3 found itself void of the intimacy of Jesus and yet, Jesus did not abandon this church. The one who was once inside the house was now standing outside on the porch knocking on the door. He was waiting for the church to welcome Him back into the place of love and intimacy. This

is the abiding Presence of God that now becomes the motivating factor for sharing His words with others. It is very clear in the Church of Corinth that the prophetic gifting and anointing was flowing strong in the church. Yet the apostle Paul writes down something that I would consider a "protocol", which would help to keep the river flowing within the banks of God's love instead of just flooding everywhere with no real direction or depth. *¹ Though I speak with the tongues of men and of angels, but have not love, I have become sounding brass or a clanging cymbal. ² And though I have the gift of prophecy, and understand all mysteries and all knowledge, and though I have all faith, so that I could remove mountains, but have not love, I am nothing. ³ And though I bestow all my goods to feed the poor, and though I give my body to be burned, but have not love, it profits me nothing. 1 Corinthians 13:1-3*

3. **God's Love builds up.** According to 1 Corinthians 14:3 the gift of prophecy will do three things in the life of the church:

    a. Strengthen, fortify, reinforce, and build up
    b. Encouragement, support, and back up
    c. Comfort, reassure, console, calm, soothe

Can you just imagine everyone in the church releasing the gift of prophecy as prescribed by the word of God in every area of the ministry?

> **Understanding the role of the Holy Spirit and the exposing of sin.**

It is easy to think that the role of a prophet or prophetic ministry is to come into the church upset and angry, exposing and calling out peoples' sins. Jesus said that after he goes back to His father that the Holy Spirit would come and it would be His job to convict the world of three things: Sin, Righteousness and Judgment. The prophetic ministry must come into alignment with the Holy Spirit and work with Him so that we are doing our part, while He does His part. It is when we break rank and start to do the

 # NOTES

the Spirit's job that people and churches are wounded. This must stop in the name of love! Jesus pointed to the disciples and said it was their job to make disciples of all nations and teach them everything that Jesus taught His disciples.

A prophet's discernment and the prophetic ability to see into the lives of others is a trust that God gives them. Can God trust you if he reveals a secret about someone's life? Many times God will reveal a weakness or even a hidden sin so that we can pray for them and see them restored in the spirit of gentleness. Those in the ministry of the prophetic will be there to build His people up and tear the works of the devil down through prayer and intercession.

When God exposes the weakness of others, this does not mean it is our job to condemn them or even convict them. It is our part to pray and intercede for them and if they are willing, bring them into a place of restoration and healing. The prophetic streams of God must not be polluted with a religious spirit of criticalness, legalism, control, bitter root judgments, or condemnation. Jesus' response to peoples' weakness was seen with a prostitute who was brought before Jesus in John 8:4-11.

God's love is unconditional for all people

Let's take a prophetic heart evaluation to see how healthy our "spiritual" heartbeat is compared with the heartbeat of God's Love. The self evaluation test on the next page is based on 1 Corinthians 13:4-7 (from the Message bible translation). Rate your level of love (within the last 7 days) on a scale of 1 to 5; **1** meaning the least amount of Love and **5** meaning the greatest amount of Love that you have shown others and the amount of love you have shown towards yourself.

GOD'S STANDARD OF LOVE	1-5 yourself	+ 1-5 others	= Total
Love never gives up			
Love cares more for others than for self			
Love doesn't want what it doesn't have			
Love doesn't strut			
Doesn't have a swelled head			
Doesn't force itself on others			
Isn't always "me first"			
Doesn't fly off the handle			
Doesn't keep score of the sins of others			
Doesn't revel when others grovel			
Takes pleasure in the flowering of truth			
Puts up with anything			
Trusts God always			
Always looks for the best			
Never looks back			
But keeps going to the end			
Total amount overall =			

This simple self-evaluation (previous page) is something you can take on a weekly basis. It will be interesting to see how it may increase or decrease in your life. Prophets and the prophetic ministry must guard their heart so that it continually matches the heartbeat of God's love.

Keep vigilant watch over your heart; **that's** *where life starts.* **Proverbs 4:23** *(MSG)*

BEGIN TO MEMORIZE THESE WORDS OF LOVE AND START TO SHARE THEM WITH OTHERS AROUND YOU.

> *"Because he has set his love upon Me, therefore I will deliver him; I will set him on high, because he has known My name. Psalm 91:14*
>
> *I drew them with gentle cords, With bands of love, And I was to them as those who take the yoke from their neck. I stooped and fed them. Hosea 11:4*
>
> *How great is the love the Father has lavished on us, that we should be called children of God! And that is what we are! 1John 3:1*
>
> *I love those who love me, And those who seek me diligently will find me. Proverbs 8:17*
>
> *He brought me to the banqueting house, And his banner over me was love. Song of Solomon 2:4*
>
> *The LORD has appeared of old to me, saying: "Yes, I have loved you with an everlasting love; Therefore with lovingkindness I have drawn you. 4 Again I will build you, and you shall be rebuilt, O virgin of Israel! You shall again be adorned with your tambourines, And shall go forth in the dances of those who rejoice. Jeremiah 31:3-4*
>
> *When I passed by you again and looked upon you, indeed your time was the time of love; so I spread My wing over you and covered your nakedness. Yes, I swore an oath to you and entered into a covenant with you, and you became Mine," says the Lord GOD. 9 Then I washed you in water; yes, I thoroughly washed off your blood, and I anointed you with oil. 10 I clothed you in embroidered cloth and gave you sandals of badger skin; I clothed you with fine linen and covered you with silk. 11 I adorned you with ornaments, put bracelets on your wrists, and a chain on your neck. 12 And I put a jewel in your nose, earrings in your ears, and a beautiful crown on your head. Ezekiel 16:8-12*
>
> *"I will heal their backsliding, I will love them freely, For My anger has turned away from him. 5 I will be like the dew to Israel; He shall grow like the lily, And lengthen his roots like Lebanon. 6 His branches shall spread; His beauty shall be like an olive tree, And his fragrance like Lebanon. Hosea 14:4-6*

– GROUP DISCUSSION –

1) Do you receive the Father's Love on a daily basis? Explain in what ways that you are receiving or not receiving the Father's love?

2) How is/was your relationship with your earthly Dad?

3) What did the unconditional test reveal about your level of unconditional love?

4) How is your measure of faith and trust in God?

 # NOTES

- ACTIVATION -

- ✓ Ask God to reveal any "father type" wounds and issues that would cause you to reject or hinder the unconditional love of God in your life.

- ✓ Jesus made a statement that helps us to Love in greater levels than we have ever loved. Jesus to him who has been forgiven loves little, but to him who has been forgiven much loves much.

- ✓ Be willing to repent of a critical spirit, false judgments, pride, or any offense against those in the body of Christ. Be willing to lay your gift at the altar and go and humble yourself before a brother or sister in Christ with the purpose of reconciliation and not revenge.

- ✓ Forgive all those including church leadership who may have hurt you knowingly or unknowingly.

- LIFE APPLICATION -

Our real ability to love God is reflected in our love for others. The Holy Spirit is the one who will help us to love unconditionally just as Jesus loves us unconditionally. Let's be true friends of God and let's remember that we are born into the family of God. There may be problems that come up between family members, but we must remember that we can walk in this life with a heart that will not choose to be offended by others.

Hidden Treasures

There are destinies hidden within every living soul that is alive on this planet, which are yet to be revealed and fulfilled. Like the diamonds that are hidden in dark, desolate and rough places of the earth; so are there "destiny diamonds" waiting to be discovered and recovered, fulfilling the word of the Lord as spoken by the prophet Isaiah. *"I'll lead you to buried treasures, secret caches of valuables-Confirmations that it is, in fact, I, God, the God of Israel, who calls you by your name".* Isaiah 45:3 (MSG) As God's chosen people we have been birthed into the kingdom for such a time as this. The global prophetic movement has already been released into deep darkness with the purpose of discovering these valuable and precious gems of glory locked inside of every human being. God has anointed you to go and call out those treasures by your words of prophecy, heart of love, and actions of grace. Go and change your world to be like Him. Jesus says "I am with you always, even unto the ends of the earth!"

God's Prophetic Declaration for all of humanity...

¹ The Spirit of GOD, the Master, is on me because GOD anointed me. He sent me to preach good news to the poor, heal the heartbroken, Announce freedom to all captives, pardon all prisoners. ² GOD sent me to announce the year of his grace— a celebration of God's destruction of our enemies— and to comfort all who mourn, ³ To care for the needs of all who mourn in Zion, give them bouquets of roses instead of ashes, Messages of joy instead of news of doom, a praising heart instead of a languid spirit. Rename them "Oaks of Righteousness" planted by GOD to display his glory. ⁴ They'll rebuild the old ruins; raise a new city out of the wreckage. They'll start over on the ruined cities, take the rubble left behind and make it new. Isaiah 61:1-4 (MSG)

NOTES

Scriptural references

Chapter 1: The secret revealed
1. Jeremiah 29:11
2. John 10:27
3. Psalms 23
4. Jeremiah 33:3
5. Luke 18:1-8
6. John 3:28-29
7. John 15:13-14
8. Matthew 7:21-23
9. Song of Solomon 1:4
10. 1 Samuel 15:24
11. Genesis 18:17-18
12. Romans 12:1-2
13. Matthew 5:10-12
14. 2 Chronicles 7:14
15. 2 Corinthians 4:7
16. Gen 50:19-21
17. 1 Corinthians 13:11-12
18. Genesis 50:19-20
19. Matthew 18:21-35

Chapter 2: The Prophetic Waves of the Holy Spirit
1. Acts 2:14-28
2. 1 Corinthians 14:20-22
3. 1 Corinthians 14:24-25
4. Luke 24:49
5. John 15:26
6. John 15:26
7. John 16:7
8. Genesis 1:4
9. Luke 1:34-35
10. Mark 16:17-20

Chapter 3: Hearing the Voice of God
1. Genesis 3:8a
2. Numbers 22:28
3. John 1:1,14
4. 2 Timothy 3:16
5. Psalms 91
6. Romans 10:8, 17
7. Ephesians 6:7,
8. 2 Corinthians 13:1
9. Acts 10:9-10
10. 2 Corinthians 10:4-5
11. Philippians 4:8
12. 1 Kings 19:11-13
13. John 21:20
14. Romans 10:17

Chapter 3: continued…
15. John 21:20
16. Psalm 46:10
17. Psalm 4:4
18. 1 Samuel 3:8
19. Matthew 3:17
20. Matthew 17:5
21. Psalm 29
22. John 16:13-14
23. Galatians 5:8
24. John 14:16-17
25. Romans 10:14-15
26. 1 Peter 4:11
27. John 10:25
28. Acts 10:38
29. John 4:10-19
30. Mark 16:17-20
31. Galatians 5:22
32. 2 Corinthians 12:2-3
33. John 4:1-2
34. Ezekiel 3:12-14
35. Acts 21:10-11
36. 2 Kings 3:15-16
37. 1 Chronicles

Chapter 4: Understanding Prophecy
1. 1 Corinthians 14:1-3
2. 1 Corinthians 14:1-5
3. Isaiah 50:4
4. Proverbs 18:21
5. 1 Kings 17:7-16
6. Ezekiel 4
7. Jeremiah 30:1-3
8. 2 Chronicles 7:14
9. John 16:13
10. John 4:1-4
11. 1 Corinthians 12:10, 14:1-5
12. Romans 12:6
13. Jeremiah 14:14
14. 2 Corinthians 11:14
15. Matthew 8:33
16. 1 John 4:1-3
17. Hebrews 1:14
18. 2 Corinthians 11:3
19. John 4:16-19

Chapter 4: Continued…

20. 1 Corinthians 14:24-25
21. 2 Chronicles 20:20-25
22. Acts 27:30-31
23. Exodus 33:15-16
24. Romans 12:6
25. Romans 10:16-17
26. Mark 11:22-24
27. Romans 1:11
28. James 2:17

Chapter 5: Sharing the Voice of God

1. Isaiah 50:4
2. Ezekiel 37:7-10
3. Isaiah 6:7-8
4. Jeremiah 25:4
5. John 4:13-19
6. Isaiah 8:18
7. Matthew 7:24-27
8. Colossians 3:23-25
9. 1 John 3:16-18
10. Jeremiah 1:17-19
11. Acts 4:18-21
12. Acts 4:23-31

Chapter 6: The Prophetic Ministry

1. Revelation 5:5
2. Acts;20:30
3. Matthew 3:17
4. Jeremiah 1:9-10
5. Isaiah 40:3-5
6. Isaiah 35:8-9
7. Hebrews 12:1-2

Chapter 7: Restoration of the Prophetic Ministry

1. Acts 3:19-21
2. 1 Samuel 10:5-13
3. Ephesians 4:11
4. Ephesians 2:19-22
5. John 14:12
6. John 4:35-36

Chapter 8: Ezekiel Prophetic River

1. Ezekiel 47
2. 1 Samuel 10:9-11
3. 1 Corinthians 12:10
4. 1 Corinthians 14:1-5
5. Romans 12:6
6. Luke 6:22-23
7. Revelation 3:21-22

Chapter 9: The Language of God's Heart

1. 1 Corinthians 13:13
2. John 3:16
3. Matthew 3:17
4. 1 Corinthians 13:1-3
5. 1 Corinthians 14:3
6. John 8: 4-11
7. 1 Corinthians 13:4-7
8. Psalms 91:14
9. Hosea 11:4
10. 1 John 3:1
11. Proverbs 8:17
12. Song of Solomon 2:4
13. Jeremiah 31:3-4
14. Ezekiel 16:8-12
15. Hosea 14:4-6
16. Isaiah 45:3
17. Isaiah 61:1-4

"MY DAILY INSPIRATIONS"

-Prophetic Journal-

"MY DAILY INSPIRATIONS"

-Prophetic Journal-

Jeremiah 33:3

What is God saying?   **Date:**

Drawing

"MY DAILY INSPIRATIONS"

"MY DAILY INSPIRATIONS"

-Prophetic Journal-

Jeremiah 33:3

What is God saying? Date:

Drawing

"MY DAILY INSPIRATIONS"

-Prophetic Journal-

Jeremiah 33:3

What is God saying? Date:

Drawing

"MY DAILY INSPIRATIONS"

-Prophetic Journal-

Jeremiah 33:3

What is God saying? Date:

Drawing

"MY DAILY INSPIRATIONS"

-Prophetic Journal-

Jeremiah 33:3

What is God saying?   **Date:**

Drawing

"MY DAILY INSPIRATIONS"

-Prophetic Journal-

Jeremiah 33:3

What is God saying?   **Date:**

Drawing

"MY DAILY INSPIRATIONS"

"MY DAILY INSPIRATIONS"

-Prophetic Journal-

Jeremiah 33:3

What is God saying? Date:

Drawing

"MY DAILY INSPIRATIONS"

-Prophetic Journal-

Jeremiah 33:3

What is God saying? Date:

Drawing

"MY DAILY INSPIRATIONS"

-Prophetic Journal-

Jeremiah 33:3

What is God saying? Date:

Drawing

"MY DAILY INSPIRATIONS"
-Prophetic Journal-
Jeremiah 33:3

What is God saying? Date:

Drawing

"MY DAILY INSPIRATIONS"

"MY DAILY INSPIRATIONS"

-Prophetic Journal-

Jeremiah 33:3

What is God saying? Date:

Drawing

"MY DAILY INSPIRATIONS"
-Prophetic Journal-
Jeremiah 33:3

What is God saying?   **Date:**

Drawing

"MY DAILY INSPIRATIONS"

-Prophetic Journal-

Jeremiah 33:3

What is God saying? Date:

Drawing

"MY DAILY INSPIRATIONS"

-Prophetic Journal-

Jeremiah 33:3

What is God saying?   **Date:**

Drawing

"MY DAILY INSPIRATIONS"

"MY DAILY INSPIRATIONS"

-Prophetic Journal-

Jeremiah 33:3

What is God saying? **Date:**

Drawing

"MY DAILY INSPIRATIONS"

-Prophetic Journal-

Jeremiah 33:3

What is God saying? Date:

Drawing

"MY DAILY INSPIRATIONS"

-Prophetic Journal-

Jeremiah 33:3

What is God saying? Date:

Drawing

"MY DAILY INSPIRATIONS"

-Prophetic Journal-

Jeremiah 33:3

What is God saying? Date:

Drawing

"MY DAILY INSPIRATIONS"

-Prophetic Journal-

Jeremiah 33:3

What is God saying? Date:

Drawing

"MY DAILY INSPIRATIONS"

-Prophetic Journal-

Jeremiah 33:3

What is God saying?   **Date:**

Drawing

"MY DAILY INSPIRATIONS"

"MY DAILY INSPIRATIONS"

-Prophetic Journal-

Jeremiah 33:3

What is God saying? **Date:**

Drawing

"BASIC TRAINING"
FOR THE PROPHETIC MINISTRY

"Global Prophetic Training" **provides basic biblical and foundational truths that will help to develop and activate your personal gifts and calling in Christ. Get ready for a journey into the prophetic realms of the Holy Spirit that will help to bring clarity, creativity and convergence in your life.**

The subject of prophets, prophecy, and prophetic ministry continues to be relevant truth for your personal life and the corporate life of the church across the globe. The promise of our heavenly Father for these "last days" is the outpouring of the Holy Spirit. The signs of this outpouring include the tangible Presence of God and prophecy. God says "I will pour out my Spirit upon all flesh and your sons and daughters will prophesy". Every believer in Christ has the ability to hear the voice of God on a daily basis. Jesus said, "My sheep hear my voice". Living a life of love, power, prosperity and productivity is linked with the simplicity of hearing the voice of God and being a doer of His word.

Through *Global Prophetic Training* you will discover:

- **How to develop the gift of prophecy and the call of prophets**
- **How to hear the voice of God**
- **How to share the voice of God**
- **How to be the voice of God**

Johnny Morales is the CEO/Owner of Dream Build Grow International is developing leaders of leaders both locally and internationally. He has served as an associate pastor and prophetic minister with Pastor Paul and Denise Goulet at the International Church of Las Vegas as well as with Jose and Toni Boveda from My Father's House church. Johnny's lifestyle of leadership, training, worship and intercession releases an awakening and reformation to today's generation. He carries the Father's heart and has a passion for God's Presence, Power, and Prophecy. Johnny's call to teach train and activate the body of Christ in productive, supernatural and fruitful ministry are evident with over 25 years of experience. This includes the local church ministry, at-risk youth ministry, prison outreach, short term missions, evangelism, marketplace ministry, conference speaking, and teaching in schools of ministry.

For more ministry & product information go to:
www.DreamBuildGrowInternational.com
johnny@DreamBuildGrow.us
602-400-8693

www.ingramcontent.com/pod-product-compliance
Lightning Source LLC
Chambersburg PA
CBHW080440110426
42743CB00016B/3225